D0128297

WILD SWEETS

from the atelier of

DOMINIQUE & CINDY DUBY

foreword by CHARLIE TROTTER

wild sweets

EXOTIC DESSERT & WINE PAIRINGS

whitecap

Copyright © 2003 by Dominique and Cindy Duby
First paperback edition published by Whitecap Books in 2006

07 08 09 10 5 4 3 2

All rights reserved. No part of this book may be reproduced, stored in a
retrieval system or transmitted, in any form or by any means, without
the prior written consent of the publisher or a licence from The Canadian
Copyright Licensing Agency (Access Copyright). For a copyright licence,
visit www.accesscopyright.ca or call toll free 1-800-893-5777.

Whitecap Books Ltd.
351 Lynn Avenue
Vancouver, British Columbia
Canada v7J 2C4
www.whitecap.ca

Library and Archives Canada Cataloguing in Publication
Duby, Dominique, 1961–
Wild sweets : exotic desserts and wine pairings / from the atelier of
Dominique and Cindy Duby.

Includes index.
ISBN 1-55285-836-7
ISBN 978-1-55285-836-3

1. Desserts. 2. Confectionery. 3. Wine and wine making.
I. Duby, Cindy, 1960– II. Title.
TX773.D8115 2006   641.8′6   C2006-902708-0

Editing by Lucy Kenward
Copy-editing by Pamela Robertson
Jacket and interior design by Peter Cocking
Jacket and interior photography by Patrick Hattenberger
Printed and bound in Hong Kong, China, by Book Art Inc., Toronto

The publisher gratefully acknowledges the financial support of the Canada
Council for the Arts, the British Columbia Arts Council, and the
Government of Canada through the Book Publishing Industry Development
Program (BPIDP) for its publishing activities.

Contents

Foreword by Charlie Trotter / 1

Introduction / 3

The Art of Presentation: The Dessert / 7

Cocktails and Canapés: The Prelude / 13

Fruit and Berries: The Woods and the Orchard / 27

Sweet and Icewines: The Dessert Matrimony / 41

Sweet Vegetables: The Garden / 75

Chocolate: The Leading Ingredient / 91

Grains and Seeds: The Fields / 119

Cookies and Chocolates: The Grand Finale / 133

The Basics / 151

Resource List / 157

About DC DUBY Wild Sweets / 158

Index / 159

Foreword

WHEN I THINK of the giants of the pastry world—the magicians, the artists—I think of Pierre Hermé, Albert Adrià and Jacques Torres, to name a few. I think of contributions so immense that our perspective on the possibilities of dessert and pastry-making becomes permanently altered. These masters, who understand and respect the tradition and history of their art, not only have the vision and the courage to see things differently, but the conviction and the energy to change them. With their extraordinary work and ideas on electrifying display in *Wild Sweets: Exotic Dessert & Wine Pairings,* Dominique and Cindy Duby have earned a place at this elite table.

This truly exceptional book completely challenges the traditional approach to what is generally regarded as the conclusion of the meal: dessert! It is as though the Dubys have gone off into the wilderness, meditated on their craft, contemplated all technique, philosophized on ingredients, forged a new perspective, and returned with an original and coherent vision of what is possible. But, as with all genuinely profound innovation, Dominique and Cindy's recipes are built on meshing the recognizable with the unthought-of. They brilliantly step "outside the box" by incorporating elements typically thought to be reserved exclusively for the savory repertoire. Szechwan pepper, black olives, red lentils, Belgian endive, celery, chanterelle mushrooms, avocado, Savoy cabbage, fennel, beets, curry, black truffles and shiso are just some of the ingredients that are deftly put to use in revolutionary new ways. And, as for their approach to technique, well I would call it a seamless mating of art and science.

Of special interest to me is the care and time that was taken to provide insightful wine notes to accompany each dish—a feature that is almost unheard of in a book about desserts. Additionally, there are sidebars throughout that are packed with important information ranging from caramelization to foaming to tempering. Plus, if that were not enough, we are treated to countless beautiful images of their stunning creations.

As a chef I am obsessed with the composition of the entire menu, and therefore I place as much importance on dessert as I do on the savoury food. *Wild Sweets* has caused me to rethink my approach to dessert, but, even more importantly, it has inspired me to re-examine all of my cuisine. Now that's a remarkable accomplishment. Three cheers to you, Dominique and Cindy—you have delivered us a masterpiece!

CHARLIE TROTTER

introduction

*Good living is an act of intelligence, by which we choose
things which have an agreeable taste rather than those which do not.*
Jean-Anthelme Brillat-Savarin (1755–1826)

———⊗———

Pastry-making is more than recipes and techniques; it is a unique blend of art and science that appeals to the senses and the emotions. For us, pastry-making is all about taste, and its purpose is to evoke emotions that will live on as unforgettable memories.

It is true that we do not eat desserts and other sweets to acquire our daily intake of vitamins and minerals; however, they contribute to our well-being at the sensory level. They provide pleasure. A moralist might say that we have to eat to live, not live to eat. Yet, as pâtissiers/chocolatiers, we know that many people still find pleasure in eating and drinking well.

Creating an unforgettable sweet experience takes time. Although many of the desserts in this book can be made relatively quickly, they are not fast foods. Preparing desserts that evoke emotion means investing effort and devoting passion for the sole purpose of providing pleasure for you and your guests. These are the memories that will last forever.

The recipes in this book are our memories, the documented account of our evolution. They are dishes inspired by the people, cultures, customs and traditions we've encountered in our international travels that have forged our philosophy and shaped our approach to pastry and chocolate design. These recipes reflect our style of desserts—the way we like to eat them, the way we like to create them and the way they evoke emotion for us.

We believe that food preparation is 60% ingredients and 40% technique; that is, the success of a dessert relies in large part on the quality of its ingredients. Prepare your desserts with the purest and finest foods at their seasonal peaks—

including as many wild foods as possible—and you are already two-thirds of your way to success. The rest depends on techniques, tricks and, most importantly, chemistry.

To turn out perfect desserts, it helps to understand something about this science. Pastry-making and chemistry are identical: they are both based on time and temperature. The basic premise is that foods exposed to heat for a certain amount of time change from a raw state to a cooked one. If you understand the stages of the process and the potential pitfalls, you can anticipate and/or prevent failure. Throughout this book, we have included information on several of the main processes so that you can confidently tackle any preparation—and yield consistently great outcomes.

We sometimes hear that nothing's really new anymore in pastry-making, that any possible recipe has already been created. We disagree. We continue to find new ways to innovate by using non-traditional exotic and wild ingredients—Szechwan pepper, salmonberries, bee pollen, Hon pears, shiso, black truffles—and emphasizing multi-dimensional tastes, such as sweet and sour and the less-common bitter and salty combination. Our desserts are full of aroma, character and intense flavours, they're light in texture and healthful in content, and they are not too sweet in taste.

Although you will need to be precise—using a scale and other measuring tools—to successfully reproduce these recipes, there is a lot of room for interpretation. We encourage you to use our recipes as starting points for your own experimentation. Substitute other ingredients if certain foods are unavailable, out of season or not to your liking. For example, if you do not like curry or you do not want to use it in desserts, replace it with cinnamon. If using chicon seems too daunting, use a braised apple instead. If you're pressed for time, just omit the décor. Or plan ahead: many of the components can be made ahead of time and stored frozen and/or in airtight containers without any loss of quality. However, never compromise on the freshness and quality of the ingredients.

Experiment too with various wines. Pastry matrimony, or the pairing of wines and desserts, also plays a big part in our dessert philosophy. Just as wines enhance savoury dishes, sweet wines complement desserts. Most of our recipes include wine suggestions. Use these as guides, and try your own pairings to determine what you like best—and to discover new and exciting possibilities.

As you read through this book, we hope that you will be inspired to recreate these recipes and to fully experience and appreciate their many pleasures. We hope too that you'll begin to experiment with your own dishes, to evoke your own emotions and to create your own memories— all it takes is a little imagination. It has been said that to be good, one must seek change. To be great, one must change often.

"All cooks, like all great artists, must have an audience worth cooking for."
ANDRÉ SIMON, FRENCH GASTRONOME

the art of presentation

The dessert

"WE EAT WITH our eyes first," says an old adage, and it means that the look of a dish is our first guide to whether we want to eat it. If it doesn't look good, we're not likely to put it in our mouths; however, if it looks good but tastes terrible that's of no benefit either. The key is balance. And the key to balanced presentation is considering three factors: 1) the design of the food itself, 2) the layout of the food on the plate, including sauces and décors, and 3) the vessel (plate or bowl) on which the food is served.

THE DESIGN

Good-looking food has an identity; it is the result of a careful creative process and it has a rationale. So the first and most important step in food design is to develop a rationale that will "tell" people what your style or philosophy is all about. Our rationale combines several design and art concepts, including classicism, modernism and minimalism.

Classicism: Our creative approach is rooted in the traditions of classic French pastry-making. At the root of many of our preparations are classic French recipes or variations.

Modernism: Although we emphasize the rich and natural flavours of classic fruit, we also highly value the exoticism that cheeses, spice infusions and unusual pastry ingredients, such as sweet vegetables and herbs, bring to the creative process. We believe in the maxim that modern desserts can be dazzling and healthful.

Minimalism: Our presentations are typically free of cumbersome and time-consuming décors. We emphasize deep and complex flavours and textures, and we stress colours and shapes so that all of the senses are stimulated, especially sound, sight and taste.

Our name, Wild Sweets, reflects our rationale: the blending of the exotic and the familiar, the element of surprise with a sense of comfort.

THE LAYOUT

Pastry-making is an art form, and, like much art, beauty is in the eye of the beholder. There is no perfect formula for creating beautiful food, but there are guidelines. Our approach to plating, the process of arranging the different food elements into a pleasing composition, is modernist. We try to evoke an emotion, rather than represent a known object or figure, with attitude and visual originality. We take into account the plate's layout and composition, the contrast of textures and the relationships among foods of different heights, shapes and colours.

Our compositions favour a minimalist architecture with groupings that are either segmented or arranged to convey a sense of unity or a broader use of space.

We give our desserts carefully crafted, clean, mostly abstract, open forms. A drizzle of sauce in the shape of an open-ended wavy line as opposed to a full circle, for example, promotes a sense of motion, which gives the whole plate a feeling of lightness.

The shapes we use in our desserts may be geometric in inspiration but not always in application. We may start with a perfect round tube, then cut a slice off the base to give it a whole new look.

The surfaces of the foods in our pastries are texturally contrasting. We combine smooth mousses with crunchy toppings and rich cakes with airy foams.

We use colours that are vibrant, varied and in harmony. Colour adds life to a composition, and some colours even evoke emotion. Red, yellow and orange are appealing food colours; blue, typically, is not.

Together, these principles contribute to desserts that not only look fantastic but also convey particular feelings.

THE VESSEL

A very important, but often neglected, aspect of food presentation is the vessel in or on which food is served. Just as food must look appealing, so must the vessel that holds it. The vessel contributes to our overall sensory evaluation of the food itself. We like to compare the presentation vessel to a painting; it has a canvas on which food is designed, components are arranged and sauces are painted, and it has a frame—the edge—that defines the area in which the art is presented. There are no rules, only guidelines to presentation.

We present our desserts on vessels that are uniquely designed. We prefer fine china, though we use glass and other materials too, and we look for plates and bowls with such features as original shapes or cavities, walls or edges of different thicknesses or with embossing.

At the same time, we try to match the shape of the vessel to the shape of the food. See, for example, how the wavy-edged plate sets off the thin, rippled vanilla cookies that garnish our simply styled white chocolate and cranberry risotto. Or how the more traditional angular plate complements the more complex but linear composition of our black pepper softcake with lemon verbena–pistachio ravioli and cherry reduction.

We also play with composing desserts that use several presentation vessels so that we can mix different shapes, sizes and materials. For example, our maple wine and cherimoya frappé with orange blossom fingers comes served in a martini glass. The clarity of the glass and its long, thin stem emphasize the lightness of the dessert; the frappé appears to be a feathery-light cloud floating high above the turbulent wavy dish filled with interesting textural elements. In contrast, the glass dish used to present our baked blue cheesecake mousse with rhubarb compote and celery confit, although similar in shape and enhancing in composition, is purely functional—it contains the foam that would otherwise run all over the plate.

For us, the most important factor in choosing china is its colour. We actually prefer no colour, that is, white only. A vessel should enhance the look of the food—make it stand out—and the combination of the vessel and the food should add to the overall visual appeal rather than detract from it. For this reason, we avoid bold colours and patterns that render the whole presentation so busy that it becomes impossible to appreciate the food.

We believe that the edge of the vessel is like the frame of a painting: you wouldn't paint on a frame, and there's no reason to place food on the edge. Why sprinkle the edge of the plate with cocoa powder when no one will eat it and when it's sure to end up all over your guests' clothing?

Although we enjoy playing with the presentation of our desserts, we must always remember that, unlike a painting, food is meant to eaten and not just looked at. We may eat with our eyes first, but the most important sense here is taste.

plating

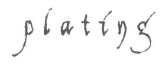

COMPOSITION. Think of your serving dish as being divided into 4 equal quarters, or quadrants. Before arranging the food on the plate, it may be helpful to make paper cutouts of the dessert components and try positioning them in different places on the plate. Be creative. Try setting the main component off to one side of the plate. Or design a "disorganized" look which fills 1 or 2 of the quadrants then drizzles only a little sauce in the remaining ones.

TEXTURE. Contrast the visual textures to make the food more appealing. Pair a silky smooth mousse with a crunchy nut croustillant. Place a bubbly chiboust beside a glossy fruit or wine reduction. Combine a crispy deep-fried beignet with a smooth and soft gelée or a creamy soup. Think about temperature too. Set a cold ice cream, for example, beside a warm bread pudding.

FORM. Shapes used in combination make for a much more complex design. Include a flatter piece such as round, square, triangle or abstract with a more three-dimensional geometric shape such as pyramid or a half sphere. Stack shapes of different textures to create height and give the dessert an airy feel, as tall desserts are often more elegant. Experiment with lines. Arrange a rectangular cake with parallel lines of sauces for a symmetrical look or offset them for a more asymmetrical approach.

COLOUR. Contrasting colours can be visually striking. If you have any doubt about which colours to combine, stick with primary colours. For example, pair a red raspberry dessert with red currants. Or with yellow lemons. Or mix two primary colours to get a complementary colour: orange apricots or mangoes. A colour chart is helpful, and so is a flavour palette.

cocktails and canapés

The prelude

———✠———

COCKTAILS AND CANAPÉS are hors d'oeuvres, generally served as the preamble to a meal. Traditionally they were savoury; small mouthfuls of food that whetted the appetite and facilitated socializing. Today many upscale restaurants serve entire dinners in this fashion: a meal is a multi-course affair with as many as five to ten dishes, small samplers served as part of a tasting menu. Instead of trying to satisfy a guest's appetite in a short time with one or two dishes, the chef teases the palate with many small courses. Each dish offers a new flavour, a different texture, a variation in temperature; and each is carefully orchestrated to surprise the diner and build the overall sensory experience.

We believe that desserts should be presented and served in the same way. For that reason, we begin with our own teasers—cocktails and canapés that can be served as the first course of a multi-dessert menu. Design your dessert menu just as you would a savoury menu: choose sweets made using different preparation techniques, textures, flavours and visual presentations. Selecting a theme can be helpful; for example, base a menu around a fruit, such as an apple or a pear, or around a season, say summer or fall. Or use a grading principle; that is, have your menu flow from light- to heavy-textured foods or delicate to strong flavours. You might start with a carrot pudding and roasted beet sauce cocktail, then follow up with dishes from the chocolate or icewine chapters, say a chocolate spring roll with mint and mango salad and a baked blue cheesecake mousse with rhubarb compote and celery confit. Or combine the cheese and dessert courses. A platter of canapés and blue cheeses is the perfect preamble—or the right finishing touch—to a cheese-based dessert such as a quince-filled maple whisky cake with goat cheese ice cream. Serve both with a few glasses of Canadian icewine.

Maple and anise French toast with lavender custard

⸺◦○○◦⸺

FRENCH TOAST

125 mL (½ cup) 2% milk

1 large egg

15 mL (1 Tbsp) Canadian maple
     whisky (or liqueur)

5 mL (1 tsp) anise powder

eight 3 cm (1¼″) cubes French bread,
     crusts on

15 g (0.6 oz) salted butter for frying

Whisk milk, egg, whisky and anise in a shallow bowl. Dip bread into the milk mixture. In a nonstick frying pan, heat butter and pan-fry bread cubes until golden brown on all sides. Keep warm until serving time.

LAVENDER CUSTARD

250 mL (1 cup) whipping cream

7.5 mL (1½ tsp) dried lavender

40 g (1.4 oz) granulated sugar

4 large egg yolks

Combine cream and lavender in a saucepan; bring to a boil. Remove from heat, cover tightly with plastic wrap to create a natural vacuum, and allow flavours to infuse for at least 15 minutes.

In a large stainless steel bowl, combine sugar and egg yolks; whisk lightly until sugar is dissolved and the mixture is a light lemon colour.

Strain cream and discard lavender. Bring cream back to a boil. Pour into the egg mixture a little at a time, whisking constantly. Place the bowl over a saucepan of simmering but not boiling water on medium heat, and whisk until the mixture reaches 85°C (185°F), or until the mixture coats the back of a spoon. Remove from heat, cool, and refrigerate until serving time.

BLUEBERRY THINS

30 mL (2 Tbsp) blueberry purée,
     page 151

35 g (1.2 oz) egg whites (about
     1 large)

5 mL (1 tsp) whipping cream

2 pinches granulated sugar

30 g (1.1 oz) rye flour

5 g (0.25 oz) corn syrup

30 g (1.1 oz) salted butter, melted

Preheat the oven to 165°C (325°F). Line a baking sheet with a silicone mat or silicone paper.

Whisk together purée, egg whites, cream, sugar, flour, syrup and butter. Trace a 3.75 cm (1½″) square onto the lid of a plastic container. Cut out the square. Place the stencil on a silicone mat, and spread the dough evenly over the hollowed part of the stencil using an offset spatula. Repeat until you have 16 thin cookies. Bake for about 5 minutes, or until golden brown. Cool. Store in an airtight container for up to 1 day.

Note: A silicone mat works better than silicone paper, which wrinkles when humid. Place soft or limp cookies in a 165°C (325°F) oven for a few minutes to crisp them.

GARNISH

8 scoops lemon sorbet, page 154

250 mL (1 cup) blueberry reduction,
     page 153

50 g (1.9 oz) fresh blueberries

8 sprigs fresh lemon thyme

ASSEMBLY

Pour 30 mL (2 Tbsp) of custard into each cocktail glass. Press a cube of warm French toast into the custard and lay a blueberry thin on top. Make sure that both are level. Place a scoop of sorbet on the thin, spoon some reduction over it, and top with a few fresh blueberries. Spike another thin into the sorbet and garnish with a sprig of lemon thyme. Serve immediately.

Serves 8

Carrot pudding with roasted beet brunoise and sauce

CARROT PUDDING

20 g (0.7 oz) salted butter
75 g (2.7 oz) granulated sugar
25 g (0.9 oz) all-purpose flour
2 large egg yolks
45 mL (3 Tbsp) carrot purée
125 mL (½ cup) whipping cream
1 large egg white

Preheat the oven to 150°C (300°F). Prepare eight 5 cm (2″) round flexible silicone moulds or spray 8 muffin tins with oil, or line 8 ramekins with butter and sugar.

In a bowl, cream together butter and sugar by hand until thoroughly mixed. Fold in flour with a spatula until combined. Add egg yolks. Slowly pour in purée, stirring constantly, until the mixture is well combined. Add cream.

In a separate bowl, whisk egg white until it forms medium peaks.

Fold egg white into the carrot mixture, making sure to combine well. Divide the batter among individual containers and bake in a bain-marie for 20 to 35 minutes, or until set. Cool slightly before unmoulding (or cool completely if using silicone moulds). Serve warm.

**ROASTED BEET BRUNOISE
AND SAUCE**

8 medium beets, unpeeled, greens removed
200 mL (¾ cup + 1 Tbsp) fruit stock, page 151
15 g (0.6 oz) granulated sugar
2.5 mL (½ tsp) powdered pectin
10 g (0.4 oz) clover honey

Preheat the oven to 180°C (350°F).

Wash beets thoroughly, but do not trim ends or peel them. Roast on a baking sheet for 40 to 60 minutes, or until beets feel soft when squeezed. Cool slightly then peel with a knife. Discard skins.

Finely dice 2 beets. Set brunoise aside for garnish.

In a food processor, purée remaining 6 beets with stock. Strain and discard solids but make sure at least 300 mL (1 cup + 3 Tbsp + 1 tsp) juice is left. Top up with fruit stock, if necessary.

In a saucepan, mix sugar and pectin. Add juice and honey, and cook until the sauce is thick and syrupy. Refrigerate until serving time.

GARNISH

8 coriander and walnut croustillants, page 156
8 scoops carrot sorbet, page 154
24 caramelized walnuts, page 156
16 carrot chips, page 156
8 sprigs fresh coriander

ASSEMBLY

Divide the brunoise evenly among 8 cocktail glasses. Pour sauce over the brunoise so it reaches just below the level of the beets, about 30 mL (2 Tbsp) per person. Place a pudding on each brunoise, top with a croustillant and a scoop of sorbet. Sprinkle sorbet with some walnuts and a few decoratively arranged chips. Garnish with sprigs of coriander. Serve immediately.

Serves 8

Rice pudding with physalis compote

RICE PUDDING AND ICE CREAM

75 g (2.7 oz) white basmati rice

290 mL (1 cup + 2 Tbsp + 2 tsp)
  2% milk

½ vanilla bean, split lengthwise

40 g (1.4 oz) granulated sugar

280 mL (1 cup + 2 Tbsp) whipping
  cream

40 g (1.4 oz) granulated sugar

2 large egg yolks

3 g (1½) gelatin leaves, bloomed

Wash rice in a strainer or colander. Rinse well with cold water until the rinse water runs clear.

In a heavy saucepan, bring rice, milk and vanilla seeds to a boil; discard vanilla pod. Reduce heat to low and cook until rice has absorbed all the liquid and grains are cooked (about 20 minutes). Once rice is cooked, stir in 40 g (1.4 oz) sugar.

Divide rice evenly between 2 bowls. Set aside.

In a saucepan, bring cream to a boil. Remove from heat.

In a stainless steel bowl, combine 40 g (1.4 oz) sugar and egg yolks; whisk lightly until sugar is dissolved. Pour cream into the egg mixture a little at a time, whisking constantly.

Place the bowl over a saucepan of simmering but not boiling water on medium heat, and whisk until the mixture reaches 85°C (185°F), or until the mixture coats the back of a spoon. Remove from heat and divide evenly between 2 containers. Set one container aside.

To one of the containers, add gelatin. Combine with the cream mixture until completely dissolved. Add to 1 bowl of cooked rice and mix well. This is the rice pudding. Pour pudding into 8 individual 5 cm (2″) round flexible silicone moulds and place in the freezer. When the outside layers of the puddings are just about frozen, about 30 to 60 minutes, unmould them. Refrigerate puddings until serving time.

Combine the second bowl of rice with the remaining container of cream. This will be the rice pudding ice cream. Transfer to a clean container with a lid and refrigerate overnight. Churn using an ice cream machine.

WILD RICE FLOUR THINS

30 mL (2 Tbsp) physalis (cape gooseberry) purée, page 151

35 g (1.2 oz) egg whites (about 1 large)

5 mL (1 tsp) whipping cream

1 pinch granulated sugar

20 g (0.7 oz) all-purpose flour

20 g (0.7 oz) wild rice flour

5 g (0.25 oz) corn syrup

30 g (1.1 oz) salted butter, melted

Preheat the oven to 165°C (325°F). Line a baking sheet with a silicone mat or silicone paper.

Whisk together purée, egg whites, cream, sugar, flours, syrup and butter. Trace a 3.75 cm (1½″) square onto the lid of a plastic container. Cut out the square. Place the stencil on a silicone mat, and spread the dough evenly over the hollowed part of the stencil using an offset spatula. Repeat until you have 16 thin cookies. Bake for about 5 minutes, or until golden brown. Cool. Store in an airtight container for up to 1 day.

Note: A silicone mat works better than silicone paper, which wrinkles when humid. Place soft or limp cookies in a 165°C (325°F) oven for a few minutes to crisp them.

PHYSALIS COMPOTE

10 g (0.4 oz) granulated sugar

0.625 mL (⅛ tsp) powdered pectin

100 mL (⅓ cup + 1 Tbsp) physalis
  (cape gooseberry) purée, page 151

5 mL (1 tsp) desert-flower honey

15 mL (1 Tbsp) tawny port

75 g (2.7 oz) physalis, finely diced

In a saucepan, mix sugar and pectin. Add purée, honey and port and cook, stirring occasionally, until the mixture is thick and syrupy. Remove from heat and stir in physalis. Cool and refrigerate.

CRISPY RICE CROQUANT

20 g (0.7 oz) crisp rice cereal

15 mL (1 Tbsp) clarified butter

15 g (0.6 oz) granulated sugar

Preheat the oven to 180°C (350°F). Line a baking sheet with a silicone mat or silicone paper.

Toss cereal with butter and sugar and mix until all grains are well coated. Spread the mixture evenly over the baking sheet. Bake for about 5 minutes, or until golden brown. Cool and store in an airtight container up to 1 week.

GARNISH

360 mL (1½ cups) cactus pear reduction, page 153, reduced to the consistency of thick soup
24 caramelized pecans, page 156
8 fresh physalises (cape gooseberries)

ASSEMBLY

Spoon about 45 mL (3 Tbsp) reduction into each cocktail glass. Place a
pudding on the reduction, making
sure that the top sticks out. Lay a
rice flour thin on the pudding and
top with a scoop of ice cream.

Spoon some compote over the ice
cream. Sprinkle with croquant and
pecans, and garnish with a physalis.
Serve immediately.

Serves 8

Spiced pineapple roast with chocolate softies

⸺ ✺ ⸺

SPICED PINEAPPLE ROAST AND JUICE

1 fresh pineapple

½ large banana, puréed or mashed

1 medium fresh mango, puréed or
    mashed

3 slices fresh ginger

60 g (2.1 oz) granulated sugar

15 mL (1 Tbsp) dark rum

125 mL (½ cup) water

1 large pinch Szechwan pepper

zest and juice of 1 lemon

15 g (0.6 oz) salted butter, melted

1 vanilla bean

Preheat oven to 180°C (350°F). Peel, core and cut pineapple into 3 cm (1¼″) cubes and place them in a 15 × 20 cm (6 × 8″) pan. In a bowl, combine banana, mango, ginger, sugar, rum, water, pepper, lemon zest and juice and butter. Split vanilla bean in half lengthwise, scrape out seeds, then add seeds and pod to the banana mixture. Pour over pineapple. Bake for about 50 minutes. Cool.

With a slotted spoon, transfer pineapple to a bowl. Set aside, but keep warm. Reserve pineapple roasting juice.

Strain roasting juice through a fine-mesh sieve; discard solids but make sure 400 mL (1½ cups + 2 Tbsp + 2 tsp) is left. Top up with fruit stock or pineapple juice, if necessary. Keep warm.

CHOCOLATE SOFTIES

125 g (4.5 oz) 70% cocoa dark
    chocolate

120 g (4.3 oz) salted butter

2 large eggs

1 large egg yolk

90 g (3.2 oz) granulated sugar

120 g (4.3 oz) all-purpose flour

Fill a medium saucepan with 5 cm (2″) water and bring to a boil. Turn off the heat but leave the pot on the burner. Combine chocolate and butter in a stainless steel bowl; place the bowl over the pan of hot water for the mixture to melt.

In a bowl, combine eggs, egg yolk, sugar and flour; whisk until well mixed. Pour chocolate into the egg mixture a little at a time, whisking constantly. Pour batter into 5 cm (2″) flexible silicone moulds and freeze.

To bake, preheat the oven to 230°C (450°F). Remove moulds from freezer and bake, still frozen, for about 2 minutes. Softies are done when they start to rise. Remove from oven and cool.

CRISPY COCONUT LEAVES

4 feuille de brick sheets (available in
    North African specialty stores, or
    substitute phyllo but it will pro-
    duce a different texture and ap-
    pearance)

100 g (3.6 oz) salted butter, melted

50 g (1.9 oz) medium shredded
    coconut

Preheat the oven to 180°C (350°F). Line a baking sheet with a silicone mat or silicone paper. Brush a feuille de brick sheet evenly with butter. Sprinkle entire feuille de brick sheet lightly with coconut. Using a cookie cutter, cut 5 cm (2″) rounds and place them on the silicone mat. Bake for about 5 minutes, or until golden brown. Cool, and store in an airtight container for up to 2 days.

VANILLA ICE CREAM

280 mL (1 cup + 2 Tbsp) 2% milk

125 mL (½ cup) whipping cream

15 g (0.6 oz) corn syrup

1 vanilla bean, split lengthwise

70 g (2.5 oz) granulated sugar

2.5 mL (½ tsp) powdered pectin

5 large egg yolks

Combine milk, cream, syrup and vanilla seeds in a saucepan; bring to a boil. Discard vanilla pod.

In a stainless steel bowl, combine sugar and pectin. Add egg yolks; whisk lightly until well mixed.

Pour the milk mixture into the egg mixture a little at a time, whisking constantly. Place the bowl over a saucepan of simmering but not boiling water on medium heat, and whisk until the mixture reaches 85°C (185°F), or until the mixture coats the back of a spoon. Cool, transfer to a clean container with a lid, and refrigerate overnight. Churn using an ice cream machine.

GARNISH

90 mL (⅓ cup + 2 tsp) raspberry–
    red pepper reduction, page 154

8 fresh raspberries

8 sprigs fresh mint

ASSEMBLY

Pour about 45 mL (3 Tbsp) pineapple roasting juice into each glass. Place a piece of pineapple in the juice, making sure that a fraction of the roast sticks out. Lay a softie on the pineapple and top with a coconut leaf. Set a scoop of ice cream onto the leaf and spoon some reduction over top. Allow reduction to drip down the sides of the ice cream. Garnish with 2 more leaves, a raspberry and a sprig of mint. Serve immediately.

Serves 8

Basic canapé dough

15 g (0.6 oz) dried yeast

200 mL (¾ cup + 1 Tbsp) water, lukewarm

350 g (12.7 oz) all-purpose flour

10 g (0.4 oz) kosher salt

15 mL (1 Tbsp) olive oil

15 g (0.6 oz) wildflower honey

Read about fermentation, page 21, before you begin.

In the bowl of an electric mixer, completely dissolve yeast in water. Add 100 g (3.6 oz) flour and mix until very sticky and runny. This mixture is called a "sponge." Scrape down the sides of the bowl with a rubber spatula and add remaining 250 g (9.1 oz) flour, covering the sponge completely and as evenly as possible. Set the bowl in a warm place (26°C/80°F) away from drafts. The sponge is ready when you see large and deep fissures forming in the flour. (These fissures mean the yeast is active and carbon dioxide is trying to escape through the flour.)

Attach a dough hook to the mixer. Add salt to the sponge and knead slowly until all ingredients are combined. Increase speed to medium and continue kneading for about 5 minutes. When the dough is smooth and shiny, pulls away from the sides, and stretches so thin you can read a newspaper through it, you have developed enough gluten and the dough is ready.

Add oil and honey to the dough and mix until combined. Turn out the dough onto a clean, lightly floured surface, cover with a clean cloth, and set in a warm place away from drafts. Allow the dough to rest, or "proof," until it doubles in size, about 30 minutes.

Punch down the dough with your fists and shape it by hand into as even a 15 × 20 cm (6 × 8") rectangle as possible. Cover again and allow to rest for another 15 minutes. Using a rolling pin, roll the dough on a lightly floured surface to a 30 × 40 cm (12 × 16") rectangle. Prick the dough all over to help it to rise as evenly as possible. Cover once again and allow to proof until it doubles in size.

To bake, preheat the oven to 200°C (400°F). Line a baking sheet with a silicone mat or silicone paper. Set dough on the mat, place in the oven, and reduce the temperature to 180°C (350°F); parbake for about 8 minutes.

ASSEMBLY

To make canapés, remove from oven, add toppings, and bake for another 8 minutes. Once baked, cool and cut into individual 2.5 × 5 cm (1 × 2") portions. Serve warm.

As an alternative, heat a barbecue on high. Lightly brush the top of the unbaked dough with olive oil and grill oil-side down for about 8 minutes. Remove from the grill, add toppings on the grilled side and grill for another 8 minutes. Cut as above and serve warm.

Yield: one 30 × 40 cm (12 × 16") loaf or 96 canapés

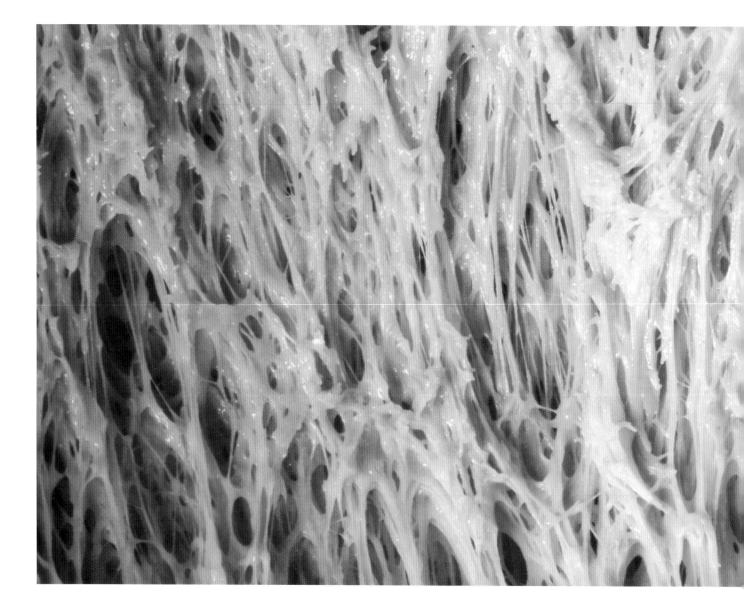

fermentation

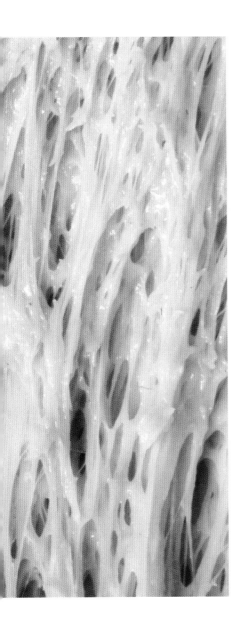

Fermentation occurs when yeast comes into contact with a sweetened solution or with the starchy sugars in flour. The yeast transforms sugar into alcohol and carbon dioxide, and gives a baked product its distinctive taste. Fermentation is complete when the dough has approximately doubled in size, which means that enough carbon dioxide gas has formed and is trapped in the flour's protein, or gluten, webs. Here are some tips for avoiding the most common fermentation pitfalls:

PRE-MIXING. Combine only the water and flour called for in the recipe. Mix them at low speed for a few minutes until a dough is formed, then let the dough rest, covered, in the mixing bowl for 20 minutes before continuing with the recipe. This pre-mixing step, called autolysis (spontaneous lysis, or rupturing of cells), reduces the total mixing time and increases the formation of gluten, which makes it easier for the dough to trap carbon dioxide.

PRE-FERMENTING. Make a small batch of dough (including the yeast) the day before you plan to use it. Refrigerate the dough overnight. The following day, make a second batch of dough and add the pre-fermented dough to it. You will achieve a better and faster fermentation and end up with a much tastier product.

CONSTANT TEMPERATURE. The magic numbers are 72°C and 160°F, the totals you should get when you add the temperatures of the water, the flour and the room. Start with water that's no warmer than 58°C (136°F) or you'll kill the yeast. Around 24°C (75°F) is best. Yeasts ferment and proof best at temperatures between 24°C (75°F) and 29°C (85°F). Ideally, the temperature of the finished dough will be 24°C (75°F). Do some quick math before you mix the yeast and water; the water temperature is the easiest to change to get your magic number of 72°C or 160°F.

TIME. Let the dough rise slowly rather than rushing the fermentation or proofing. The slower the process at a lower temperature, the better the end result.

front to back: Fennel confit, lemon and almond canapé *(p. 23);* Apricot, cherry and pistachio canapé *(p. 23);*
Fig, orange and walnut canapé *(p. 23);* Apple, apricot and pine nut canapé *(p. 23);*

Wild canapé toppings

—⊶⊷—

APPLE, APRICOT AND PINE NUT TOPPING

3 Golden Delicious apples, peeled, cored and cut in 0.5 cm (¼″) dice

30 mL (2 Tbsp) olive oil

200 mL (¾ cup + 1 Tbsp) fruit stock, page 151

150 g (5.3 oz) raisins

½ sprig rosemary

100 g (3.6 oz) good-quality, store-bought firm apricot jelly

100 g (3.6 oz) pine nuts, toasted

Combine apples, oil, stock, raisins and rosemary in a covered pot; braise until apples are soft and raisins have absorbed most of the liquid. Spread jelly over parbaked bread base. Arrange the apple mixture on top and sprinkle with pine nuts. Bake or grill for about 8 minutes. Cool. Cut into 2.5 × 5 cm (1 × 2″) portions. Serve warm or cold.

Yield: 96 canapés

FIG, ORANGE AND WALNUT TOPPING

200 mL (¾ cup + 1 Tbsp) fresh orange juice, page 151

150 g (5.3 oz) dried figs, each fig cut into 8 even pieces

30 mL (2 Tbsp) olive oil

zest of 2 oranges

15 mL (1 Tbsp) anise seeds

4 fresh oranges, peeled, seeded, segmented and halved

140 g (5 oz) walnut pieces, toasted

Combine juice, figs, oil, zest and anise seeds in a saucepan. Cook until almost all the liquid is evaporated. Add orange sections and cook for 1 minute to allow flavours to blend (oranges must remain firm). Cool.

Arrange figs and oranges over parbaked bread base and sprinkle with walnuts. Bake or grill for about 8 minutes. Cool. Cut into 2.5 × 5 cm (1 × 2″) portions. Serve warm or cold.

Yield: 96 canapés

APRICOT, CHERRY AND PISTACHIO TOPPING

300 g (10.8 oz) dried apricots, cut into 0.5 cm (¼″) dice

150 g (5.3 oz) dried cherries, quartered

15 g (0.6 oz) fresh ginger, finely grated

300 mL (1 cup + 3 Tbsp + 1 tsp) orange juice, page 151

300 mL (1 cup + 3 Tbsp + 1 tsp) fruit stock, page 151

60 mL (¼ cup) olive oil

200 g (7.2 oz) pistachios, chopped

Combine apricots, cherries, ginger, juice, stock and oil in a saucepan. Cook until liquid is evaporated and fruit is soft and plump. Cool.

Arrange fruit over parbaked bread base. Sprinkle with pistachios and bake or grill for about 8 minutes. Cool. Cut into 2.5 × 5 cm (1 × 2″) portions. Serve warm or cold.

Yield: 96 canapés

FENNEL CONFIT, LEMON AND ALMOND TOPPING

60 mL (¼ cup) olive oil

2 fennel bulbs, halved

zest and juice of ½ lemon

15 g (0.6 oz) wildflower honey

30 mL (2 Tbsp) fennel seeds

300 mL (1 cup + 3 Tbsp + 1 tsp) fruit stock, page 151

140 g (5 oz) whole natural almonds, toasted and chopped

Combine oil, fennel bulbs, lemon zest and juice, honey, fennel seeds and stock in a saucepan. Braise until fennel is cooked (the tip of a knife penetrates the flesh easily) and the liquid has evaporated. Cool.

Cut fennel into 0.5 cm (¼″) slices and arrange over parbaked bread base. Sprinkle with almonds. Bake or grill for about 8 minutes. Cool. Cut into 2.5 × 5 cm (1 × 2″) portions. Serve warm or cold.

Yield: 96 canapés

coagulation

Coagulation is the operation of changing the liquid form of an egg (whole, yolk or white) into a solid form by exposing the egg to heat. As the proteins in the egg cook, they lose moisture, shrink and become firm. The resulting product is termed a "denatured" protein. Time and temperature directly affect the result of the process. The most common problems encountered when making egg-based preparations such as custards are curdling and incomplete thickening. Here are a few preventative tips:

LOW HEAT. Curdling is the result of too long an exposure to high heat, which causes most of the water in the protein to be squeezed out. An egg-based custard or anglaise sauce starts to set at 71°C (160°F) but will curdle above 85°C (185°F). To prevent curdling, cook custards over low heat. When baking custards, puddings, flans or steamed meringues in the oven, set the cooking dish in a bain-marie (water bath) so that the heat is dispersed more evenly. When cooking crème anglaise and other egg-based desserts on the stove, place them in a stainless steel bowl or a small saucepan over a double boiler so that no part of the egg is directly exposed to high heat.

PROPER RATIOS. Egg-based preparations like custards and puddings contain other products such as milk and/or cream. If there is too much of these other liquids relative to the amount of egg, the dessert will not set properly and you'll end up with a thin, runny product. Typically, two whole eggs per 250 mL (1 cup) of liquid is the minimum for proper thickening. Watch the amount of sugar (15% to 20% of the total mixture is standard); too much sugar can slow down or prevent custards setting.

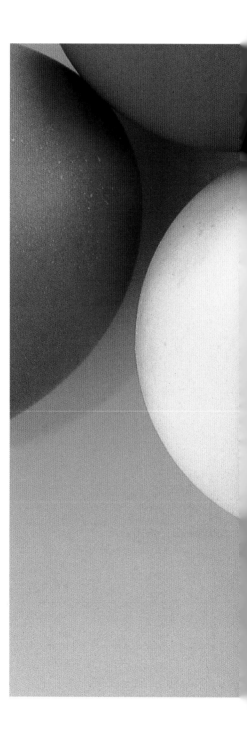

fruit and berries

The woods and the orchard

———⌘———

O F WILD FOODS, it has been said that there are few new raw ingredients
coming from the sea, woods and garden—there are just new ways to use
them. We believe that wild fruit and berries remain largely underused in sweet
baked goods. How often have you seen a dessert made with barberry, cowberry,
dewberry, olallieberry, thimbleberry or youngberry?

Wild fruit and berries typically pop up only in farmers' markets and at certain times of the year. And that's not a bad thing. For the most part, we like to
emphasize fresh seasonal foods; eating and creating with wild fruit and berries
means that we can only make certain desserts in season. But it's worth it: wild
varieties add a whole new range of flavours. Taste a wild alpine strawberry and
you'll savour a sweet aroma that's stronger than perfume and a flavour that
lingers on your tongue for what seems like forever.

Wild fruit contains much less water than most of its cultivated counterparts,
which is one of the reasons that wild fruit has more flavour. Try to use wild food
whenever possible; however, if this is not possible, use a dry-heat cooking
method, such as roasting, baking or pan-frying, to evaporate the water and concentrate the natural flavours. Try this with pears, apples or nectarines, for
instance, and you'll end up with a shrunk fruit full of natural flavour and sugar.

Because of their lower water content, wild fruit and berries typically freeze
well, and this conservation method is a great way to stock up and have access to
wild fruit year-round. For berries, discard any stems, leaves and/or any inedible
parts of the fruit, brush off any dirt, lay the fruit flat on a tray, and freeze. Once
frozen, pack the berries into small, heavy-duty sealable bags or, for best results,
vacuum seal them. Freezer life is typically one year under good conditions
($-18\,^{\circ}$C/$0\,^{\circ}$F).

Orange and basil soup,
alpine strawberry compote and mascarpone mousse

———⊗⊗⊗———

WHAT COULD BE MORE SUMMERY than fruit salad? This simply presented dessert can be made nearly year-round, but it is especially good made with fresh summer produce. Sweet sun-ripened wild strawberries combine with fragrant home-grown basil and a little cream to put a new spin on the flavour and texture of this classic dessert. *Serves 6*

ORANGE AND BASIL SOUP

250 mL (1 cup) orange juice,
   page 151
4 to 6 basil leaves, shredded
60 g (2.1 oz) granulated sugar
4 g (2) gelatin leaves, bloomed
   Combine juice, basil and sugar in a saucepan; heat but do not boil. Add gelatin, stirring to combine. Remove from heat, cover tightly with plastic wrap to create a natural vacuum, and allow flavours to infuse at room temperature for at least 10 minutes. Strain, discard basil, and allow mixture to cool at room temperature up to about 2 hours. Do not allow it to set.

ALPINE STRAWBERRY COMPOTE

22 g (0.8 oz) granulated sugar
2 mL (⅓ tsp) powdered pectin
160 mL (⅔ cup) alpine or field strawberry purée, page 151
15 mL (1 Tbsp) lemon juice
105 g (3.8 oz) fresh alpine or field
   strawberries, hulled and
   finely diced

In a saucepan, mix sugar and pectin. Add purée and juice. Bring to a boil and cook until the mixture is thick and syrupy. Remove from heat and allow it to cool. Add strawberries and refrigerate until serving time.

MASCARPONE MOUSSE

100 mL (⅓ cup + 1 Tbsp) whipping
   cream
15 g (0.6 oz) granulated sugar
½ vanilla bean, split lengthwise
3 g (1 ½) gelatin leaves, bloomed
30 g (1.1 oz) mascarpone cheese
130 mL (½ cup + 1 tsp) whipped
   cream (in soft peaks)
   Scald whipping cream with sugar, vanilla seeds and pod in a heavy saucepan. Remove from heat and discard vanilla pod. Add gelatin and stir to combine. Add cheese and, using a whisk, mix until well combined. Cool the mixture to 20°C (68°F). Fold in whipped cream. Serve immediately.

GARNISH

3 fresh oranges, peeled, seeded and
   segmented
6 basil leaves, cut into thin strips
12 coriander and orange oil
   gaufrettes, page 138

ASSEMBLY

Mix orange segments with basil. Fill each cocktail glass ⅓ full with this mixture. Cover completely with soup and refrigerate until set. Pour a layer of compote over the soup and spoon on some mousse just before serving. Serve immediately with 2 gaufrettes on the side.

WINE

Sweet sparkling wines such as Canadian VQA sparkling icewine, Italian Moscato d'Asti or Asti Spumante should pair well with the fresh fruit lightness and prevalent orange flavours of this dessert. Another option is a Californian Essensia.

Concord grape clafoutis with sweet Savoy cabbage and warm grapes

⸺⣿⣿⣿⣿⣿⣿⣿⣿⣿⣿⣿⣿⣿⣿⣿⣿⣿⣿⣿

INSPIRED BY A DESSERT of the famed Michelin 3-star chefs at Troisgros, this dish combines simple preparation with complex taste. Omit the tuiles and this dessert is ready in minutes and without a lot of mess. But what a dessert it is! Sweet and crunchy cabbage contrasts with luscious warm custard-like clafoutis, and both are perfectly balanced with the natural acidity of the Concord grape. *Serves 8*

CONCORD GRAPE CLAFOUTIS
45 mL (3 Tbsp) crème fraîche
5 large egg yolks
70 g (2.5 oz) granulated sugar
20 g (0.7 oz) all-purpose flour
120 g (4.3 oz) Concord grapes
 Preheat the oven to 165° C (325° F).
 Combine cream, egg yolks and sugar in a bowl; whisk until thoroughly combined. Fold in flour. Pipe or spoon this mixture into 5 cm (2″) oval flexible silicone moulds (or buttered individual ramekins). Top with grapes and bake for about 15 minutes. Unmould and keep warm until serving time.

BASIC TUILES
75 g (2.7 oz) unsalted butter, softened
75 g (2.7 oz) icing sugar
1.25 mL (¼ tsp) pure vanilla extract
80 g (2.9 oz) egg whites (just less than 3 large), at room temperature
75 g (2.7 oz) all-purpose flour
 Cream butter, sugar and vanilla in a bowl. Slowly add egg whites, making sure that each addition is well incorporated before adding more. Gently fold in flour until just combined. Do not overmix. Store in an airtight container and refrigerate until needed.

 To bake, preheat the oven to 180° C (350° F). Trace a football shape onto the lid of a plastic container. Cut out the football. Place the stencil on a silicone mat, and spread a layer of dough about 2 mm (⅛″) thick evenly over the hollowed part of the stencil. Remove stencil and, using a decorating comb with square ends (cut pointed tips out of a regular decorating comb to make ends square), draw parallel lines 2 mm (⅛″) apart inside the football and leaving the outer edges of the football uncut. Bake for 4 to 6 minutes. Allow to cool and store in an airtight container.
 Note: If the tuiles have absorbed too much humidity, crisp them by baking them for a minute or so in the oven. The dough can also be refrigerated for several days or frozen for several months. For best results, thaw frozen dough in the refrigerator overnight before using.

SWEET SAVOY CABBAGE
20 g (0.7 oz) unsalted butter, melted
100 g (3.6 oz) Savoy cabbage, cut into fine julienne strips
2.5 mL (½ tsp) granulated sugar
 Place butter in a microwaveable bowl and heat on high for 30 seconds to 1 minute until very hot. Add cabbage and sugar, and toss well. If cabbage is too crunchy, place the bowl

of cabbage in a microwave oven and cook briefly. Serve immediately.

WARM CONCORD GRAPES
15 g (0.6 oz) unsalted butter
16 Concord grapes, halved and seeded
 Place butter in a microwaveable bowl and heat on high for 30 seconds to 1 minute until very hot. Toss with grapes. Serve immediately.

GARNISH
10 mL (2 tsp) bee pollen
125 mL (½ cup) warm Concord grape reduction, page 153

ASSEMBLY
Mound cabbage in the centre of each plate and sprinkle with a few grains of bee pollen. Place a warm clafoutis on cabbage and top with a tuile. Arrange grapes around the plate and drizzle reduction around the dessert and over grapes. Serve immediately.

WINE
A Muscat wine, which is one of the few wines that actually taste like grapes, should pair well with the leading fresh grape flavour of this dessert. A Moscato d'Asti is one suggestion.

Cherry-almond blancmange over frangipane and crème fraîche soup

BLANCMANGE is a time-honoured French classic. Our modern version retains the traditional creamy texture but contrasts it with roasted almonds and creamy yet crunchy almond frangipane. Cherries, rosehip and crème fraîche provide acidity to set off the sweetness. All in all, a great new classic! *Serves 6*

CHERRY-ALMOND BLANCMANGES

30 g (1.1 oz) dried cherries, finely chopped
22.5 mL (1½ Tbsp) kirsch
60 g (2.1 oz) granulated sugar
½ vanilla bean, split lengthwise
330 mL (1¼ cups + 2 Tbsp) whipping cream
90 mL (⅓ cup + 2 tsp) whole milk
6 g (3) gelatin leaves, bloomed
100 g (3.6 oz) ground almonds, roasted golden brown

Line 5 cm (2″) metal ring moulds with strips of acetate or waxed paper, set on a metal baking sheet, and place in freezer for at least 30 minutes, or until very cold.

Soak dried cherries in kirsch until fruit absorbs most of the liquid. Set aside.

Combine sugar, vanilla seeds, cream and milk in a saucepan; bring to a boil. Remove from heat and add gelatin. Cool the mixture over an ice-water bath.

Remove moulds from freezer. Cover the bottom of each mould with a thin layer of the cream mixture. Allow cream to set.

Fold cherries into the remaining cream mixture. Divide evenly among moulds. Freeze blancmanges until hard.

Remove from moulds and peel off acetate or waxed paper. Cut 1.25 cm (½″) from one side of each. Stand blancmange on this flat edge and allow to thaw about 4 hours in the fridge. Roll in almonds.

ALMOND AND CHERRY FRANGIPANE

140 g (5 oz) almond cream, page 155
70 g (2.5 oz) pastry cream, page 155
100 g (3.6 oz) sour cherries, pitted

Preheat the oven to 165° C (325° F). Line a 15 cm (6″) square pan with silicone paper.

Combine almond and pastry creams in a bowl. Spread the mixture evenly in the pan and cover completely with cherries. Bake for about 40 minutes. Cool.

Remove frangipane from pan, and freeze for about 1 hour, or until firm. Cut frozen frangipane into 3.75 × 5 cm (1½ × 2″) slices. Allow frangipane to thaw 1 to 2 hours (in the fridge), or until soft, before serving.

ROSE WATER TUILES

45 g (1.6 oz) bread flour
45 g (1.6 oz) cake flour
85 g (3.1 oz) icing sugar
90 g (3.2 oz) egg whites (about 3 large)
1.25 mL (¼ tsp) rose water, or to taste
60 g (2.1 oz) unsalted butter, melted
few drops of liquid red food colouring (note that a fat-soluble or candy food colouring works best)

Sift flours and sugar in a large bowl. Using a rubber spatula, incorporate egg whites, stirring well to make sure there are no lumps. Add rose water and butter, and mix well. Stir in food colouring and combine until the mixture is uniformly coloured. Transfer to a plastic container with a tight-fitting lid and refrigerate until needed, or up to 1 week.

To bake, preheat the oven to 180° C (350° F). Spread a thin even layer of dough onto a silicone mat to a thickness of 2 mm (⅛″). Using a decorating comb with square ends (cut pointed tips out of a regular decorating comb to make ends square), draw parallel lines 7.5 cm (3″) long. (Use a disposable plastic piping bag if you do not have a decorating comb. Cut a hole in the tip and pipe parallel lines.) Bake for 4 to 6 minutes. Cool and store in an airtight container.

Note: A silicone mat works better than silicone paper, which wrinkles when humid.

CRÈME FRAÎCHE SOUP

125 mL (½ cup) whipping cream
5 mL (1 tsp) kirsch
10 g (0.4 oz) vanilla sugar
60 mL (¼ cup) crème fraîche

Just before serving, combine cream, kirsch, sugar and crème fraîche in a bowl. Beat lightly with a whisk and serve immediately.

GARNISH

80 mL (⅓ cup) rosehip gelée, page 153, refrigerated in a shallow container

zest of 1 lime, freshly grated

ASSEMBLY

Lay a slice of frangipane in the centre of a soup plate. Set a blanc-mange, cut-side down, on top. Pour enough soup around the dessert to cover the base of the plate. Using the tip of a teaspoon, break off small chunks of gelée and arrange them around dessert. Sprinkle gelée with zest. Just before serving, spike some tuiles into blancmange. Serve immediately.

WINE

Sweet sparkling wines such as Canadian VQA sparkling icewine or Italian Moscato d'Asti or Asti Spumante should pair well with the lightness of the blancmange and the soup.

churning/overrun

Churning is the operation of freezing a mixture using a batch freezer. While churning, the machine incorporates air into the mixture to increase volume (a process called overrun) and prevent ice crystals from developing. The amount of overrun is affected by the type and speed of the ice cream machine, the length of time the mixture is being churned, the fullness of the machine (half full is best) and the formulation of the mixture being frozen. For example, if you start with 1 L (4 cups) of ice cream mixture (typically called "custard") and the overrun ratio is 80%, you will end up with 1.8 L (about 7 cups). The best ice creams have between 10% and 30% overrun.

A quality ice cream has a smooth texture without large ice crystals and a light, creamy smooth consistency that is neither sandy nor gritty. Here are some tips for preventing the most common churning problems:

FORMULATION. The custard that forms the base of the ice cream mixture should be well balanced, with the perfect ratio of milk solids (at least 20%), fats (at least 10%) and sugars (typically around 15%). Select recipes from tested sources only.

MATURING. Refrigerate the custard overnight so that it can mature. The protein in the custard will swell and bind with the water, which yields a product with a much smoother texture and more intense flavour.

FRIDGE TEMPERATURE. Start churning the custard at a temperature between -3°C (27°F) and 1°C (35°F). A lower temperature will result in large crystals; a higher one may cause the cream in the custard to turn to butter.

ADDING SUGAR. Sugar lowers the freezing point of water, which keeps the ice cream soft enough to eat, even when it's cold. Honey is twice as effective as sugar, so try substituting 20% honey for some of the sugar; that is, if the recipe calls for 100 g (3.6 oz) sugar, try 20 g (0.7 oz) honey and 80 g (2.9 oz) sugar.

ADDING ALCOHOL. Alcohol lowers the freezing point of water too. If you add alcohol, use less sugar, or use the regular amount of sugar but enjoy a softer ice cream.

Crèmes renversées with crabapple beignets and cassis-caramel sauce

⎯⎯⎯∞∞∞⎯⎯⎯

CRABAPPLES are a great dessert fruit. Their miniature size allows for wonderful presentations and their natural tartness balances sweeter fruit. Here, stuffed with brown sugar, raisins and spices, slow roasted then lightly coated in a beer batter, they become incredible morsels of buttery soft and sweet flesh with a delightfully thin yet crunchy shell. Served with a creative variation on crème caramel, this dish is a simple and impressive late-summer treat. *Serves 6*

CRÈMES RENVERSÉES

160 mL (⅔ cup) whole milk
40 g (1.4 oz) granulated sugar
2 large eggs

Preheat the oven to 150°C (300°F).

Scald milk. In a bowl, combine sugar and eggs. Pour milk into the egg mixture a little at a time, whisking constantly. Fill 5 cm (2″) ceramic ramekins or round flexible silicone moulds with cream to a depth of 2 cm (¾″). Bake in a bain-marie for 35 minutes, or until the custard is set. Cool completely, then refrigerate for at least 4 hours (overnight is better). Run a knife around the sides (for ceramic moulds only) and unmould as close to serving time as possible.

CRABAPPLE BEIGNETS

12 crabapples
juice of 2 fresh lemons
14 g (0.5 oz) raisins
14 g (0.5 oz) walnuts
2.5 mL (½ tsp) garam masala
5 mL (1 tsp) brown sugar
2.5 mL (½ tsp) dry yeast
85 mL (⅓ cup + 1 tsp) beer
pinch of granulated sugar
50 g (1.9 oz) all-purpose flour
pinch of salt
olive oil, in a pump, for spraying
1 L (4 cups) oil for deep-frying

Preheat oven to 150°C (300°F). Lightly spray a baking pan with oil.

Cut tops off crabapples, rub tops with juice, and reserve. Using a small melonball cutter or a paring knife, core the apples, making sure to keep the fruit whole.

In a food processor, pulse raisins, walnuts, garam masala and brown sugar to form a paste. Completely fill the crabapples with this mixture. Put the tops back on crabapples. Place crabapples in pan and spray lightly with oil. Cover with aluminum foil and bake for about 30 to 35 minutes. Cool.

To make the batter, combine yeast with beer and granulated sugar in a bowl; stir until yeast dissolves completely. Add flour then salt and mix well. Allow to stand at room temperature for about 1 hour.

Heat a deep fryer to 180°C (350°F) just before serving time. Remove tops from crabapples. Set aside. Using a fork or skewer, dip crabapples in batter. Drop in hot oil and fry until golden brown. Drain on a paper towel for a few seconds. Replace tops. Serve immediately or keep warm in a 120°C (250°F) oven for a few minutes.

CASSIS-CARAMEL SAUCE

150 g (5.3 oz) granulated sugar
50 mL (3 Tbsp + 1 tsp) corn syrup
50 mL (3 Tbsp + 1 tsp) water
100 mL (⅓ cup + 1 Tbsp) cassis (black currant) purée, page 151

Before making this sauce, read about caramelization on page 123. Combine sugar, syrup and water in a saucepan; cook over high heat until the mixture is caramel in colour. Remove from heat and decook with purée. If sauce is too runny, return to heat and cook until sauce is thick and syrupy. Refrigerate.

APPLE CHIPS

125 mL (½ cup) cassis (black currant) purée, page 151
2 small Golden Delicious apples

Preheat the oven to 50–60°C (100–125°F) or prepare a food dehydrator.

Pour purée into a small dish.

Cut apples into 24 paper-thin slices. Dip slices on both sides into purée, allow excess to drip off and place on a silicone mat or silicone

paper to dry in an oven (or place on trays in a food dehydrator). In the oven, bake for about 1 hour, or until all moisture has evaporated and apples are dry. Store in an airtight container.

ASSEMBLY

Pipe or spoon a bead of coulis in the centre of each plate. Place a crème renversée in the centre and top with a few apple chips. Arrange a beignet on each side of the crème renversée. Serve immediately.

WINE

A Canadian VQA Vidal icewine or French botrytis-affected Chenin Blanc such as Quarts de Chaume should work well with the predominant flavours of apples and the creaminess of the custard in this dessert. Vin Santo may be another option.

Creamy avocado pudding with pink grapefruit reduction and candied zest

─⊶⊷─

AVOCADOS are so naturally creamy that, when puréed, they can easily replace butter in desserts. This avocado pudding, made from avocados and crème fraîche, redefines the terms rich and smooth. Paired with a fresh pink grapefruit reduction, which adds tartness, and grapefruit sorbet, which provides cool citrusy notes, this is an enticingly refreshing dessert. *Serves 8*

AVOCADO PUDDING

30 g (1.1 oz) salted butter
180 g (6.4 oz) granulated sugar
125 g (4.5 oz) avocado flesh (about
    ¾ avocado)
3 large egg yolks
125 mL (½ cup) whole milk
125 mL (½ cup) crème fraîche
juice and zest of 1 lime
1.25 mL (¼ tsp) nutmeg, freshly
    grated
90 g (3.2 oz) all-purpose flour
60 g (2.1 oz) egg whites (about
    2 large)

Preheat oven to 150°C (300°F). Spray 8 muffin tins with oil or use 5 cm (2″) round flexible silicone moulds, or line 8 ramekins with butter and sugar.

In a food processor, cream butter and sugar. Add avocado and egg yolks, and combine until the mixture is smooth. Pour in milk, cream, juice, zest and nutmeg, and process well. Add flour and mix as briefly as possible, until just incorporated. Do not overmix.

In a separate bowl, whisk egg whites until they form soft peaks.

Fold egg whites into the avocado mixture with a rubber spatula, making sure to combine them well. Divide batter among individual containers and bake in a bain-marie for 35 to 40 minutes, or until lightly

golden brown and springy to the touch. Cool slightly before unmoulding (or cool completely if using silicone moulds). Serve warm, or refrigerate and reheat in a microwave oven about 1 to 2 minutes, or just until warm before serving.

CANDIED GRAPEFRUIT ZEST

100 g (3.6 oz) granulated sugar
100 mL (⅓ cup + 1 Tbsp) water
zest of 2 grapefruits (as much white
    pith removed as possible)
500 mL (2 cups) oil for deep-frying

Combine sugar and water in a saucepan; bring to a boil. Pour the syrup over zest and transfer to an airtight container. Refrigerate overnight.

To cook, preheat a deep fryer to 190°C (375°F). Remove any last pieces of white pith from zests and discard. Pat zests dry and fry until lightly golden brown. Remove from oil with a slotted spoon and drain briefly on a paper towel. Cool.

GARNISH

2 pink grapefruits, peeled, seeded
    and segmented
8 lemon and mint oil sucrées,
    page 137, cut into 3 × 4.5 cm
    (1¼ × 1¾″) rectangles
8 scoops or quenelles pink grapefruit
    sorbet, page 155
125 mL (½ cup) pink grapefruit
    reduction, page 153
455 g (16.4 oz) pink grapefruit emul-
    sion, page 152

ASSEMBLY

Place a warm pudding slightly off centre on each plate. Top with a few pieces of zest. Arrange a few segments of grapefruit in front of pudding, top with a rectangle of sucrée, and finish with a scoop or quenelle of sorbet. Drizzle some reduction over the grapefruit and spoon emulsion on either side of the dessert. Serve immediately.

WINE

Pairing acidic desserts, especially grapefruit ones, is very difficult. However, ripe pink grapefruit is typically less acidic and sweeter, and therefore somewhat easier to pair, than its yellow relative if it appears in a dessert made of creamy, sweet ingredients. Muscat wines such as Muscat de Rivesaltes, a Canadian VQA late-harvest or American late-harvest Riesling icewine will tolerate the acidity and should pair well with the predominant creamy flavours of the custard. A Sauternes or late-harvest Sauvignon may be other suggestions.

sweet and icewines

The dessert matrimony

———◦◦◦———

THE END of a perfect meal requires just the right dessert, not to mention the right dessert wine. But how does one determine that perfect pairing of food and wine?

The first and most important rule is that there are no rules. Tastes vary: one person's perfect match is another's hideous marriage. Yet the great fun of food and wine pairing is that the combinations are endless—and experimentation is the key to new discoveries!

THE LEADING CATEGORIES OF SWEET WINE

Late-harvest wines: Made from grapes left on the vine after the usual harvest time. These grapes contain a higher amount of residual sugar and produce sweeter wines.

Botrytis-affected wines: Made from grapes that have been infected with a mould (*Botrytis cinerea,* also known as noble rot) that draws moisture from the fruit. These grapes contain concentrated sugar and the mould imparts a distinct and appealing flavour to the wines.

Fortified wines: Wines in which alcohol has been added to the "must," the freshly pressed grape juice, to stop the fermentation and maintain a high natural sugar content. Typically, these wines contain between 15% and 20% alcohol by volume.

Sparkling wines and champagnes: Made using several techniques, including a laborious and expensive multi-step process called méthode champenoise, which uses a second fermentation stage and over 100 manual operations. A mixture of sugar and spirits, called dosage, is added just before the final corking and determines how sweet the sparkling wine or champagne will be. For dessert, choose

the demi-sec (3.3% to 5% sugar) and doux (over 5% sugar) sparkling wines or champagnes. Or try a crémant, which is less effervescent and "creamier" textured than other sparkling wines.

ICEWINES

Made from grapes that have been left on the vine to freeze. Freezing draws out the grapes' moisture and concentrates the sugar and the flavour, which produces a very sweet wine. Authentic icewines are known as eiswein in Germany and as vQA icewine in Canada (see page 43).

SOME LESS-COMMON CATEGORIES OF SWEET WINE

The French call wines made from grapes that have been dried on the vine before harvesting to concentrate their natural sugars by the name *passerillé.* Wines made from grapes harvested then left to dry on racks or straw sheets in the sun before processing are called *vin de paille,* literally "straw wine." In Italy, both passerillé wines and vin de paille are called *passito.* Rancio and maderized are wines that were deliberately allowed to oxidize, typically in wooden barrels and/or by exposing them to air and/or heat.

Although some people prefer to contrast the flavour of the wine with the dessert, we choose wines that will enhance the flavours of our desserts. We suggest that you try to match certain flavours in the wine with similar characteristics in the food. For example, the peach overtone of a Riesling, the honey note in Sauternes or ginger and apricots in Gewürztraminer are best paired with lighter, similar fruit-based desserts. Likewise, the darker, coarser light caramel overtone in port, nutty flavour in sherry and dried-fruit taste in Banyuls are better served with rich nutty or chocolate-based desserts.

Pairing wines with food requires balance. If one is too strong, it may reduce or mask the flavour of the other rather than enhancing it. An ideal combination adds a new dimension to your taste perception, and each element alters the flavours of the other. Try to keep in mind not just the primary ingredient of the food or wine but also the secondary ones. For example, sometimes the spices or sauces determine the best-suited wine.

Each variety of grape, and hence each wine, has certain characteristic flavours.

Cabernet Franc: primary fruit aromas, strawberries and cream, rhubarb and figs, currants, raspberries and blackberries. Example: Canadian Niagara Peninsula VQA red icewines

Chardonnay: tropical fruit, butterscotch, vanilla and citrus. Example: Late-harvest and botrytis-affected from California

Chenin Blanc: ripe fruit, apples and dried apricots. Examples: French Quarts de Chaume, Bonnezeaux, Coteaux du Layon

Ehrenfelser: dried apricots, apples, honey and papayas. Example: Canadian Okanagan Valley VQA icewines

Gewürztraminer: ginger, cinnamon, pineapples, apricots, cloves, roses, lychees, grapefruit and fruit salad. Example: Sélection de Grains Nobles from the French Alsace

Muscat: grapes, oranges, roses and musky scents. Examples: sparkling Italian Moscato d'Asti, fortified French Beaumes-de-Venise, Californian Essensia and black muscat

Pinot Blanc: ripe pears, apples, hint of cinnamon, lemons, bananas, figs and strawberries. Example: Canadian Okanagan Valley VQA icewines

Riesling: fresh apples, peaches, tropical fruit, orange peel, honey and candied ginger. Examples: Auslesen, Beerenauslesen, Trocken-beerenauslesen and Eisweine from Austria and Germany, and late-harvest from California

Sauvignon Blanc: (almost always blended with Sémillon) citrus, honey, vanilla, apricots and peaches. Example: botrytis-affected French Sauternes and Californian late-harvest and botrytis-affected

Vidal: mangoes, lychees, passion fruit and ripe pineapples. Example: Canadian Niagara Peninsula VQA icewines

Viognier: ripe peaches, flowering citrus, apricot and orange marmalade, spicy clove and caramel. Example: Passito-style late-harvest from California, late-harvest Condrieu from France

Zinfandel: black pepper, ripe berries such as cherries and blackberries, raisin and vanilla. Example: Californian port-style fortified wines

Although there are many sweet wines to choose from, our favourite is definitely Canadian VQA icewine. Initially, it is intensely sweet and flavourful in the mouth; then its acidity creates a clean, dry finish to the taste. Strictly controlled by VQA (Vintners Quality Alliance) regulations that prohibit any artificial freezing of grapes, this exceptional wine is made from grapes that are left on the vine well into December and January. The grapes for Canadian icewine are painstakingly picked by hand in their naturally frozen state, sometimes in the middle of the night, and ideally at temperatures of -10°c to -13°c. The frozen grapes are pressed in the extreme cold. Much of the water in the juice remains frozen as ice crystals during the pressing, and only a few drops of sweet concentrated juice are salvaged. The juice is then fermented very slowly for several months. Yields are very low—often as little as 5% to 10% of the wine produced from unfrozen grapes—which is one of the reasons for icewine's higher price. Try these desserts with icewine and discover why it is considered one of the wine world's best-kept secrets and winter's gift to the wine lover.

Apricot-and-chanterelle wonton with tamago roll and plum sauce

TAMAGO, LITERALLY "EGG" in Japanese, is a sweetened omelet that is typically rolled and served on top of sweet sushi rice. Here it is flavoured with ginger and sesame oil. Served with a light summer fruit salad, it becomes a simple dessert. Accompanied by a crispy wonton filled with creamy apricot-and-chanterelle custard and dressed with soft poached plums and zesty Japanese plum wine sauce, it becomes a symphony of exotic flavours and textures. *Serves 8*

APRICOT-AND-CHANTERELLE WONTON

10 g (0.4 oz) dried chanterelles
125 mL (½ cup) hot water
30 g (1.1 oz) dried apricots, finely diced
385 g (13.5 oz) pastry cream, page 155
5 mL (1 tsp) amaretto, or to taste
four 20 cm (8") square spring roll wrappers, quartered into 10 cm (4") squares
1 large egg, beaten, for egg wash
1 L (4 cups) vegetable oil for deep-frying

Place chanterelles in water in a microwaveable container with a lid; bring to a boil. Remove container immediately and allow chanterelles to sit, covered, until they have doubled in size. Drain chanterelles, reserving liquid. Squeeze excess water from chanterelles, adding it to reserved cooking liquid. Finely chop chanterelles and set aside.

Place apricots in chanterelle water. Rehydrate in a microwave oven as for chanterelles; allow to sit, covered, until doubled in size. Drain apricots, reserving liquid for plum sauce (below). Set aside.

Combine cream, chanterelles, apricots and amaretto, and mix until thoroughly combined.

Brush each spring roll wrapper completely with egg wash. Spoon a dollop of cream filling in the centre of the wrapper. Fold 2 opposite corners to the centre then repeat with the other 2 corners. Squeeze all edges tightly to form a pyramid. Repeat until all wrappers and filling are used up. Freeze for at least 1 hour, or until needed (store in an airtight container for longer periods). The wontons will keep frozen for 2 to 3 weeks.

To bake, preheat the oven to 150° C (300° F). Heat a deep fryer to 180° C (350° F). Drop frozen wontons in hot oil and fry until golden brown. Remove from oil with a slotted spoon and lay wontons on a wire rack over a baking sheet. Place in the oven for 5 minutes, or until hot in the centre. Keep warm until serving time.

Note: This recipe makes 12 to 16 wontons. Do not try to make smaller amounts; just serve one more per person or freeze for later use.

TAMAGO ROLL

4 large eggs
60 mL (¼ cup) 2% milk
pinch of fleur de sel
15 g (0.6 oz) granulated sugar
1.25 mL (¼ tsp) ground ginger
5 mL (1 tsp) sesame oil
olive or vegetable oil for spraying

Combine eggs, milk, fleur de sel, sugar, ginger and sesame oil; whisk until well combined.

Heat a rectangular tamago frying pan or a regular nonstick frying pan over medium heat. Remove from heat, spray lightly with oil, and pour a small amount of batter into the pan. Swirl batter so that it covers the bottom of the pan in a thin layer. Cook 1 side only until lightly browned. Remove from heat. Starting from the bottom edge, roll the omelet into a tight cylinder. Cut into 5 cm (2") pieces. Keep warm until serving time.

PLUM SAUCE

10 g (0.4 oz) granulated sugar
2.5 mL (½ tsp) powdered pectin
5 mL (1 tsp) lemon zest
60 mL (¼ cup) chanterelle-apricot cooking liquid (see above)
10 g (0.4 oz) buckwheat honey
160 mL (⅔ cup) apricot purée, page 151
30 mL (2 Tbsp) Japanese plum wine

In a saucepan, mix sugar and pectin. Add zest, cooking liquid, honey and purée. Bring the mixture to a boil, stirring well, and cook until it is thick and syrupy. Strain, and cool to body temperature. Add wine. Refrigerate until serving time.

POACHED PLUMS

8 yellow plums, unpeeled but pitted
50 mL (3 Tbsp + 1 tsp) plum eau de vie (or brandy)
500 mL (2 cups) simple syrup, page 152

Sterilize a 600 mL (20 oz) mason jar and tight-fitting lid in a hot water bath.

Bring water to a boil in a small saucepan. Blanch plums for about 30 seconds, remove from water with a slotted spoon, and place them in the mason jar. Pour eau de vie over plums.

Bring syrup to a boil in a small saucepan. Pour over plums and eau de vie, filling the mason jar to the rim. Seal the jar immediately and turn it upside down once. Cool then refrigerate overnight.

GARNISH

4 shiso leaves, halved

ASSEMBLY

Pour a small amount of sauce into each side dish. Place a plum on top. Wrap a tamago roll in a shiso leaf and centre on the front of each plate. Cut wonton in half and place half on either side of the roll. Place the side dish on the plate. Serve immediately.

WINE

Canadian VQA Riesling icewine or American late-harvest Riesling should match well with the predominant flavours of apricot and egg in this dessert.

Icewine gelée with coconut milk sabayon and pumpkin seed croquant

⟨⟨⟨

SUCCESSFULLY PAIRING a dessert with wine is a great experience—but eating your wine is even better! This elegant dessert is based on simple, clean flavours. Barely set with gelatin, the icewine gelée is perfectly matched with the tropical flavours of juicy lychees, a silky smooth coconut milk sabayon and a fresh coconut salad. *Serves 8*

ICEWINE GELÉE

60 mL (¼ cup) fruit stock, page 151
6 g (3) gelatin leaves, bloomed
375 mL (1½ cups + 1 Tbsp) icewine
   (late-harvest may be substitted)
8 fresh lychees, peeled and pitted

Heat stock in a microwave oven on high for about 45 seconds to 1 minute. Add gelatin and stir until dissolved. Cool to body temperature and add icewine.

Place a lychee in the bottom of each 90 mL (3 oz) glass and cover completely with the icewine mixture. Refrigerate to set, 1 to 2 hours, and until serving time.

COCONUT MILK SABAYON

5 large egg yolks
45 g (1.6 oz) granulated sugar
180 mL (¾ cup) coconut milk

Combine egg yolks, sugar and milk in a stainless steel bowl. Place the bowl over a saucepan of simmering but not boiling water on medium-low heat, and whisk constantly until the mixture reaches 85°C (185°F) and is thick and foamy. Cool to room temperature and set aside.

COCONUT SALAD AND HONEY DRESSING

250 mL (1 cup) fruit stock, page 151
6 g (0.3 oz) clover honey
1 fresh young coconut, shaved and
   thinly sliced
zest of 1 lime, finely grated

Bring stock to a boil in a saucepan. Reduce stock to about ¼ of its original volume. Add honey and cool to room temperature.

Toss coconut with zest and sweeten to taste with honey dressing. Refrigerate at least 1 hour to allow flavours to blend. Serve cold.

PUMPKIN SEED CROQUANT

100 g (3.6 oz) hot caramel décor,
   page 156
75 g (2.7 oz) pumpkin seeds, toasted

Using a spoon, drizzle caramel in figure 8's on a silicone mat or silicone paper. Immediately sprinkle seeds over top. Work quickly so that sugar is still liquid when placing seeds, otherwise they will not adhere. Break into pieces before serving.

ASSEMBLY

Place a glass of gelée on one side of each serving dish. Mound some salad in front of the glass and drizzle a little dressing around the fruit. Garnish salad with a croquant. Just before serving, spoon some sabayon on gelée. Serve immediately.

WINE

The secret to a perfect wine pairing is to use the wine you want to pair as an ingredient in the recipe. As this dessert already contains a large amount of unprocessed wine, it does not really need pairing. However, should you want to, an icewine or late-harvest would be the best option.

Date mousse pound cake with caramelized apricots and icewine foam

———⊶⊷⊶———

DRIED FRUIT is distinctly more concentrated than fresh in its perfume and flavour. This sandwich dessert combines an extraordinarily smooth dried date mousse with moist thin slices of pound cake. Crystallized mint leaves make a side of greens and a plump date acts as the pickle. A cold creamy apricot soup, incredibly light icewine foam and caramelized apricots vary the texture and the temperature. Substitute dried figs or fresh fruit if dried dates are not available. *Serves 8*

DATE MOUSSE

100 mL (⅓ cup + 1 Tbsp) 2% milk
50 g (1.9 oz) dried dates, finely
  chopped
15 g (0.6 oz) granulated sugar
2 large egg yolks
4 g (2) gelatin leaves, bloomed
100 mL (⅓ cup + 1 Tbsp) whipped
  cream (in soft peaks)

Scald milk in a saucepan. Pour over dates, cover tightly with plastic wrap to create a natural vacuum, and refrigerate overnight.

Purée the date mixture in a food processor until smooth. Transfer to a microwaveable bowl and heat to just below the boiling point.

In a stainless steel bowl, combine sugar and egg yolks; whisk lightly until sugar is dissolved. Pour date purée into the egg mixture a little at a time, whisking constantly.

Place the bowl over a saucepan of simmering but not boiling water on medium heat, and whisk until the mixture is thick and foamy. Remove from heat and add gelatin, stirring well to combine. Cool to 20°C (68°F) and slowly fold in cream using a rubber spatula. Refrigerate until set.

POUND CAKE

1 large egg
3 large egg yolks
5 mL (1 tsp) orange blossom water
5 mL (1 tsp) water
125 g (4.5 oz) salted butter, softened
125 g (4.5 oz) granulated sugar
100 g (3.6 oz) cake flour, sifted

Preheat the oven to 180°C (350°F). Line a 15 cm (6″) square pan with silicone paper.

Combine the egg, egg yolks and waters in a bowl. Set aside.

Using an electric mixer, cream softened butter and sugar until light and fluffy. With the motor running, slowly pour in the egg mixture and mix until thoroughly incorporated. Using a rubber spatula, fold in flour until just combined. Do not over-mix. Pour the batter into the pan and bake for 40 to 50 minutes, or until a toothpick inserted in the centre of the cake comes out clean. Unmould and cool on a wire rack.

Slice cake into thin and even layers, about 5 mm (¼″) thick. Spread date mousse evenly between layers. Freeze. Cut cake into 3 cm (1¼″) squares and thaw before serving.

CANDIED DATES

8 dried dates
125 mL (½ cup) simple syrup,
  page 152

Combine dates and syrup in a microwaveable container with a lid; bring to a boil. Allow to soak, covered, at room temperature for a couple of hours then refrigerate overnight, or until dates are completely rehydrated.

ICEWINE FOAM

15 mL (1 Tbsp) simple syrup,
  page 152
2 g (1) gelatin leaf, bloomed
100 mL (⅓ cup + 1 Tbsp) icewine

Heat syrup in a saucepan. Remove from heat and add gelatin, stirring well to combine. Add icewine. Pour the liquid into a siphon cream dispenser and add nitrous oxide. Refrigerate for a couple of hours.

CARAMELIZED APRICOTS

60 g (2.1 oz) granulated sugar
2 fresh apricots, pitted and quartered

Pour sugar into a shallow bowl. Press apricots cut-side down into sugar.

Heat a nonstick pan and dry roast the sugared sides until they are a light caramel colour. Remove from heat and keep warm until serving time.

APRICOT SOUP

250 mL (1 cup) apricot purée,
      page 151
60 g (2.1 oz) granulated sugar
4 g (2) gelatin leaves, bloomed

Combine purée and sugar in a saucepan. Heat to just below the boiling point. Remove from heat and add gelatin, stirring well to combine. Cover and allow to sit at room temperature for 10 minutes. Half fill shot glasses with soup and refrigerate until set.

GARNISH

16 crystallized mint leaves, page 156

ASSEMBLY

Place a square of cake in the centre of a sectioned plate. Top with a candied date and 2 mint leaves. Just before serving, dispense about 15 mL (1 Tbsp) of foam into a small dish and top with a wedge of apricot. Place the dish of foam on one side of the cake and a shot glass of soup on the other. Top soup with some foam and serve immediately.

WINE

A Canadian VQA icewine, French Sauternes or lesser-known Barsac or late-harvest American Riesling should pair well with the leading apricot and date flavours of this dessert.

Exotic fruit salad with guava sauce and phyllo galettes

⸻⸎⸻

THE MÉLANGE of exotic fruit and flavours in this salad works very well. However, you could also use seasonal fruit in place of or in addition to the ones suggested here. Whichever fruit you choose, this salad is quick and easy to make and is wonderfully refreshing after lunch or as the first course on a dessert menu. *Serves 8*

EXOTIC FRUIT SALAD
¼ pineapple, trimmed, peeled and
    cored
8 strawberries, hulled
1 small mango, peeled and pitted
1 small pepino, peeled and seeded
¼ honeydew melon, peeled and
    seeded
½ horned melon (kiwano), fleshy
    seeds only
1 small pomegranate, seeds only

Thinly slice pineapple, strawberries, mango, pepino and honeydew melon to a thickness of 2 mm (⅛″). Combine fruit in a large bowl. Toss in horned melon and pomegranate seeds and serve immediately.

Note: To prepare this salad up to a couple of hours ahead, refrigerate each sliced fruit in an individual bowl. Toss together before serving.

GUAVA SAUCE
55 g (2 oz) granulated sugar
3.75 mL (¾ tsp) powdered pectin
250 mL (1 cup) water
100 mL (⅓ cup + 1 Tbsp) guava
    purée, page 151
1 vanilla bean

In a saucepan, mix sugar and pectin. Add water and purée. Split vanilla bean in half lengthwise, scrape out seeds, then add seeds and pod to the purée mixture. Bring the mixture to a boil, stirring well, and cook until it reaches the consistency of soup. Discard vanilla pod. Cool and refrigerate until serving time.

PHYLLO GALETTE
454 g (1 lb) box phyllo sheets, frozen
100 g (3.6 oz) unsalted butter,
    melted, or more
50 g (1.9 oz) granulated sugar

Preheat the oven to 180°C (350°F). Remove protective paper or plastic layers from a roll of phyllo. Keeping the roll tightly folded, slice 2 mm (⅛″) strips from the end of the roll with a sharp serrated bread knife. Use ¼ of the roll and wrap and return the rest to the freezer.

Place butter in a shallow bowl. Toss strips with butter, making sure that phyllo is completely coated. Add sugar and toss again. Spread phyllo evenly across a silicone mat. Place another mat on top and flatten phyllo to as thin a layer as possible, about 2 mm (⅛″), with a rolling pin. Bake for 5 to 10 minutes, or until phyllo is golden brown. Cool and break into equal-sized galettes. Store in an airtight container.

STRAWBERRY CROQUANT
50 mL (3 Tbsp + 1 tsp) strawberry
    purée, page 151
50 g (1.9 oz) corn syrup
50 g (1.9 oz) granulated sugar
50 g (1.9 oz) all-purpose flour
50 g (1.9 oz) unsalted butter, melted

Preheat the oven to 160°C (320°F). Line a baking sheet with a silicone mat.

Combine purée, syrup, sugar, flour and butter, in that order, mixing well after each addition.

Using the back of a spoon, spread about a teaspoon of dough onto a silicone mat, making a 7.5 cm (3″) circle. Repeat to make 8 circles. Leave at least 2 finger spaces between each croquant. Bake about 5 minutes, or until bubbly and golden brown. Cool on mat. Remove carefully and store in an airtight container.

Note: The dough can be refrigerated for several days or frozen for several months. For best results, thaw frozen dough in the refrigerator overnight before using.

GARNISH
8 scoops or quenelles guava sorbet,
    page 154

ASSEMBLY
Arrange an assortment of fruit and seeds in the centre of each dish. Pour sauce around the salad. Place a galette on the salad. Top with a scoop or a quenelle of sorbet and garnish with a piece of croquant. Serve immediately.

WINE
A Canadian VQA sparkling icewine or good quality Asti Spumante should match the lightness and exotic flavours of this salad.

Quince-filled maple whisky cake with goat cheese ice cream

⎯⎯⎯ ⎯ ∞∞∞ ⎯ ⎯⎯⎯

THE MOST NORTH AMERICAN OF DESSERTS is without a doubt apple pie à la mode. Quince gives that classic a new twist. Firmer textured than an apple, quince tastes like a cross between an apple and a pear. When cooked, quince becomes wonderfully soft and exudes an incredibly potent aroma. Encased in a crispy maple whisky–flavoured crust and accompanied by creamy goat cheese ice cream, this unique creation contains all the heat, cold and crunch of the original. *Serves 8*

MAPLE WHISKY CAKE

210 g (7.6 oz) all-purpose flour
50 g (1.9 oz) granulated sugar
1.25 mL (¼ tsp) ground cinnamon
zest of ¼ lemon
10 mL (2 tsp) Canadian maple
    whisky (or liqueur)
50 mL (3 Tbsp + 1 tsp) cold water
1 large egg
20 g (0.7 oz) salted butter, melted
1 L (4 cups) vegetable oil for deep-
    frying

Combine flour, sugar, cinnamon and zest in a large bowl. Make a well in the middle.

In a separate bowl, combine whisky, water and egg, mixing well. Pour the whisky mixture into the well. Add butter, mixing until ingredients form a dough. Do not over-mix. Shape the dough into a ball, wrap in plastic wrap, and refrigerate for at least 1 hour.

Heat a deep fryer to 180°C (350°F). Place dough on a floured surface and and roll it to a thickness of about 1.25 cm (½"). Cut into 5 cm (2") squares. If you like, score the top of the dough, making a check-ered pattern with a sharp knife. Drop squares in hot oil and fry until golden brown, about 2 to 3 minutes. Remove from oil with a slotted spoon, drain on a paper towel for a few seconds, and cut in half horizon-tally to make a top and a bottom. Keep warm until serving time.

QUINCE COMPOTE

500 mL (2 cups) fruit stock, page 151
60 mL (¼ cup) lemon juice
120 g (4.3 oz) granulated sugar
1 large cinnamon stick
2 large quince

Combine stock, juice, sugar and cinnamon in a saucepan; bring to a boil then remove from heat.

Peel, core and cut each quince into 8 wedges. Cut each wedge in 5 mm (¼") dice. Drop quince imme-diately into the stock mixture to minimize oxidation. Cook, covered, over medium heat until fruit is soft but still retains its shape. Remove quince with a slotted spoon, reserv-ing cooking juice, and set aside.

Strain cooking juice into a sauce-pan. Reduce cooking juice until it has the consistency of honey, about 20 to 30 minutes. Add quince to the syrup and keep warm until serving time.

GOAT CHEESE ICE CREAM

100 mL (⅓ cup + 1 Tbsp) whipping
    cream
150 mL (½ cup + 2 Tbsp) 2% milk
150 g (5.3 oz) soft goat cheese
100 g (3.6 oz) granulated sugar
1.25 mL (¼ tsp) powdered pectin
3 large egg yolks

Scald cream and milk in a sauce-pan. Add cheese, stirring well to dis-solve.

In a stainless steel bowl, combine sugar and pectin. Add egg yolks; whisk lightly until well mixed.

Place the bowl over a saucepan of simmering but not boiling water on medium heat. Pour the cheese mix-ture into the egg mixture a little at a time, and whisk constantly until the mixture reaches 85°C (180°F), or until the mixture coats the back of a spoon. Cool over an ice-water bath, then transfer to a clean container with a lid and refrigerate overnight.

Churn using an ice cream machine. Spread ice cream in a pan to a depth of 2 cm (¾"). Freeze.

Cut frozen ice cream into 5 cm (2") squares. Cut each square in half diagonally to make 2 triangles. Keep frozen until serving time.

MAPLE WHISKY SAUCE

190 mL (¾ cup + 2 tsp) apple purée,
    page 151
15 mL (1 Tbsp) maple syrup
6 g (0.3 oz) unsalted butter
30 g (1.1 oz) granulated sugar
15 mL (1 Tbsp) water
15 mL (1 Tbsp) Canadian maple
    whisky (or liqueur)

Combine purée, syrup and butter in a small bowl.

Combine sugar and water in a saucepan; cook over high heat until the mixture is caramel in colour. Remove from heat and decook with the apple mixture. Return to heat, and cook until sauce is thick and

syrupy. Stir in whisky. Keep warm until serving time.

SESAME GLASS
100 g (3.6 oz) corn syrup
15 g (0.6 oz) sesame seeds
8 g (0.3 oz) black sesame seeds

Preheat the oven to 180°C (350°F).

Dip a 5 cm (2″) wide painter's brush in syrup and paint a rainbow-shaped strip about 10 cm (4″) wide on a silicone mat. Sprinkle lightly with sesame seeds and bake for about 5 minutes.

Cool strip for about 30 seconds. Lift the warm glass with a spatula and mould into a funky shape with a flat base. Cool completely, then store in an airtight container. Use the same day.

ASSEMBLY
Place the bottom half of a square of cake in the centre of each plate. Cover cake with compote and top with a triangle (or a scoop) of ice cream. Place the other half of the cake on top. Garnish with a sesame glass décor and spoon sauce around cake. Serve immediately.

WINE
A Canadian VQA icewine, French Sauternes or American late-harvest should match well with the predominant flavours of quince, cinnamon and cheese in this dessert.

Wine pairing

Pairing wines can be difficult. Not all sweet wines are dessert wines, and not every dessert can be matched with a sweet wine. Experiment to determine what you like best—and discover for yourself how a well-chosen wine can enhance a suitably prepared dessert. Here are some tips:

SWEETNESS. The wine must be sweeter than the dessert. If the dessert is sweeter, the wine will taste thin and uninteresting.

ACIDITY. Citrus fruit, such as lemons, limes and grapefruits, are difficult to pair with wine because the acidity of the fruit dominates and hides the characteristic of the wine.

COLD. Use frozen elements only as a complement to a main dessert. Ice cream and sorbets numb the tongue and wash out the flavours of most sweet wines.

CHEMICAL REACTIONS. Consume one tannin at a time. Serve a chocolate dessert *or* a wine rich in tannins, not both. Paired they will create an unpleasant, astringent, bitter sensation in the mouth.

BALANCE. Match the wine to the occasion. Make desserts that are rich in flavour yet not heavy in texture. Match the weight of the wine and the dessert; for example, a rich icewine with a rich pudding or mousse. Provide sweet and acidic contrast but in moderation. Read about the personalities of different wines and use them to either contrast or enhance flavours. In some cases, opposites will attract.

Chestnut moelleux with slow-roasted Fuji apples and pear tempura

—⊱⊰—

THE INGREDIENTS and techniques of this playful dish are definitely Japanese in origin. The Fuji apples, slow roasted to a sensual softness, contrast beautifully with the crispy pear tempura. The creamy and comforting chestnut moelleux adds a definitive European flair, but the succulently sweet carrot and plum sauce, Japanese plum wine–soaked raisins and delicate shiso amplify the Asian notes of this incredible dessert. *Serves 8*

CHESTNUT MOELLEUX

180 mL (¾ cup) whipping cream
25 g (0.9 oz) granulated sugar
2 large egg yolks
40 g (1.4 oz) chestnut paste (available at specialty food stores)
2 g (1) gelatin leaf, bloomed

Line 4 cm (1¾″) metal ring moulds with strips of acetate or waxed paper, set on a metal baking sheet, and place in freezer for at least 30 minutes, or until very cold.

Scald cream. Combine sugar, egg yolks and paste in a stainless steel bowl. Place the bowl over a saucepan of simmering but not boiling water on medium heat. Pour cream into the egg mixture a little at a time, and whisk constantly until the mixture reaches 85°C (185°F), or until the mixture coats the back of a spoon. Remove from heat and add gelatin. Cool the mixture over an ice-water bath.

Remove moulds from freezer. Cover the bottom of each mould with a thin layer of the cream mixture. Allow cream to set in the freezer. Once set, divide remaining cream evenly among moulds. Refrigerate until set. Keep refrigerated until serving time or freeze in an airtight container for up to 2 weeks.

PEAR TEMPURA

1 egg yolk
250 mL (1 cup) ice-cold water
15 mL (1 Tbsp) Japanese plum wine
140 g (5 oz) all-purpose flour
1.25 mL (¼ tsp) Chinese five-spice powder
pinch of baking soda
2 small Anjou pears
1 L (4 cups) oil for deep-frying

Combine egg yolk, water and wine in a large bowl; whisk well.

Sift together flour, five-spice powder and baking soda. Slowly add the flour mixture to the egg mixture, making sure that all ingredients are thoroughly combined. Pour into a shallow bowl.

Heat a deep fryer to 180°C (350°F) just before serving time. Cut pears into 1.25 cm (½″) thick slices. Discard the cores. Cut wider slices in half lengthwise. Immediately drop slices into the batter and remove, draining excess batter. Drop in hot oil and fry until golden brown. Drain on a paper towel for a few seconds. Serve immediately or keep warm in a 100°C (200°F) oven for a few minutes.

CARROT AND PLUM SAUCE

55 g (2 oz) granulated sugar
3.75 mL (¾ tsp) powdered pectin
250 mL (1 cup) carrot purée
100 mL (⅓ cup + 1 Tbsp) plum purée, page 151
60 mL (¼ cup) Japanese plum wine
1 vanilla bean

In a saucepan, mix sugar and pectin. Add purées and wine. Split vanilla bean in half lengthwise, scrape out seeds and add them to the purée mixture. Discard vanilla pod. Bring the mixture to a boil, stirring well, and cook until it reaches the consistency of soup. Cool and refrigerate until serving time.

SLOW-ROASTED FUJI APPLES

2 small Fuji apples
15 mL (1 Tbsp) grapeseed oil
20 g (0.7 oz) granulated sugar
30 mL (2 Tbsp) Japanese plum wine

Preheat oven to 150°C (300°F).

Wash and halve apples. Remove and discard cores. Cut apples into 1.25 cm (½″) wedges and rub them with oil, making sure that they are well coated. Place them in a 22.5 cm (9″) square ovenproof dish.

Combine sugar and wine in a bowl, then pour over apples. Cover the dish with aluminum foil and bake for about 30 minutes, or until apples are soft but still retain their shape. Keep warm until serving time.

continued overleaf

PLUM WINE–POACHED RAISINS

80 g (2.9 oz) golden raisins

190 mL (¾ cup + 2 tsp) Japanese
  plum wine

Combine raisins and wine in a
microwaveable container with a lid;
heat on high for 30 seconds. Shake
well. Repeat three more times, shak-
ing well after each heating. Allow to
soak, covered, at room temperature
for several hours, or until raisins
have absorbed all or most of wine.

PEAR SALAD

1 medium Anjou pear

15 mL (1 Tbsp) citrus dressing,
  page 153 (optional)

Using a Japanese turning slicer,
cut pear into long spaghetti-like
strands. Toss pear with dressing, if
you like. Prepare just before serving
so pear stays crisp and white.

GARNISH

24 carrot chips, page 156

4 shiso leaves, halved with scissors
  then each ½ halved again

ASSEMBLY

Pour 45 mL (3 Tbsp) sauce into each
bowl. Place a moelleux in the centre.
Alternate 2 slices each of apple and
pear on top of moelleux. Arrange a
few raisins around the dessert. Decorate with chips, a few strands of
salad and a couple of strips of shiso.
Serve immediately.

WINE

A Canadian VQA icewine, American
late-harvest or French Botrytis affected Chenin Blanc should pair well
with the tree fruit and creamy chestnut custard flavours of this dessert.

Pear and icewine compote with smoked mango fillet and sweet pea shoot salad

⁓⁓⁓

LET YOUR IMAGINATION RUN WILD with this dazzling dessert. Imagine buttery soft pears in a luscious icewine compote. Picture perfectly ripe sweet mangoes lightly smoked with aromatic Szechwan pepper then topped with a crispy fresh sweet pea shoot salad tossed with citrus-vanilla dressing. This is the ultimate in gustatory adventure. *Serves 8*

PEAR AND ICEWINE COMPOTE

250 mL (1 cup) fruit stock, page 151
1 large Anjou pear, peeled, cored and
    cut in 1.25 cm (½″) dice
4 g (2) gelatin leaves, bloomed
90 mL (⅓ cup + 2 tsp) icewine

Bring stock to a boil in a saucepan. Reduce heat to medium, add pears and cook, covered, until fruit is soft but still retains its shape, about 10 to 20 minutes. Remove pears from stock with a slotted spoon and set aside to cool.

Reduce stock to 100 mL (⅓ cup + 1 Tbsp). Remove from heat and add gelatin, stirring well to combine. Cool to 20°C (68°F) and stir in icewine and pears. Pour compote into a shallow nonstick pan and refrigerate until set.

SPICED SMOKED MANGO FILLETS

70 g (2.5 oz) jasmine rice (or other
    white rice)
15 mL (1 Tbsp) Szechwan pepper
15 mL (1 Tbsp) anise seeds
1 large mango, unpeeled but pitted

Combine rice, pepper and anise seeds in a wok or a heavy cast-iron pan; heat on high until the mixture starts to smoke. Remove from heat. Cover smoking rice and spices with loose aluminum foil; lay mango on top. Cover the wok or pan with a tight-fitting lid or a bowl, making as tight a seal as possible. Allow mango to smoke for 10 to 15 minutes, according to taste. Remove mango from pan, skin it, and slice it into thin fillets. Discard rice, pepper and anise seeds.

MANGO GRATIN

80 g (2.9 oz) pastry cream, page 155
60 mL (¼ cup) mango purée,
    page 151
20 g (0.7 oz) mascarpone cheese

Combine cream and purée in a microwaveable bowl; heat on high in 15-second intervals. Stir between intervals. Repeat until the mixture is warmed and thoroughly combined. Fold in cheese. Keep warm until serving time.

PEA SHOOT SALAD

50 g (1.9 oz) sweet pea shoots,
    leaves only
60 mL (¼ cup) citrus dressing,
    page 153

Just before serving, gently toss pea shoots with dressing, making sure that all leaves are coated.

GARNISH

8 sesame seed and almond croustil-
    lants, page 156, cut in 5 cm (2″)
    rounds and baked in 5 cm (2″)
    round flexible silicone moulds
80 mL (⅓ cup) sweet pea emulsion,
    page 152

ASSEMBLY

Arrange some compote in the centre of each plate. Top with a croustillant and a few mango fillets. Spoon a dollop of gratin on the fillets and caramelize with a blowtorch (or heat a metal spatula over an open gas flame and slide it over the gratin). Place a small bunch of salad atop the gratin. Spoon a bead of emulsion in front of the dessert. Serve immediately.

WINE

Here is another opportunity to use the wine you want to pair as an ingredient in the recipe. A Selection de Grains Nobles (SGN) from the French Alsace should pair well with the spice notes of this dessert.

Black pepper softcake with lemon verbena-pistachio ravioli and cherry reduction

———— ∞∞∞ ————

ALTHOUGH THIS DESSERT may look rather daunting, it is actually quite simple. Many of the components can be made ahead of time and assembled very quickly just before serving. If you omit the chocolate squares and use store-bought pasta, this wonderful early-summer dessert will be ready in no time. Crispy pasta is filled with a luscious pistachio emulsion scented with lemon verbena and topped with juicy, ripe Bing cherries. A moist and buttery black pepper softcake adds substance and unexpected heat. *Serves 8*

BLACK PEPPER SOFTCAKE

250 g (9.1 oz) white chocolate

30 mL (2 Tbsp) apple purée, page 151

60 g (2.1 oz) unsalted butter

75 g (2.7 oz) sweetened condensed milk

75 g (2.7 oz) all-purpose flour

50 g (1.9 oz) ground almonds

2.5 mL (½ tsp) black pepper, or to taste

4 large eggs

Preheat the oven to 190°C (375°F).

Fill a medium saucepan with 5 cm (2″) water and bring to a boil. Turn off the heat but leave the pot on the burner. Combine chocolate, purée and butter in a stainless steel bowl; place the bowl over the pan of hot water for the mixture to melt. Add milk and stir well.

Using a whisk, combine flour, almonds, pepper and eggs in a bowl. Fold in the chocolate mixture. Pour batter into a 15 × 20 cm (6 × 8″) non-stick pan. Bake for about 15 to 20 minutes. Remove from oven, cool and cut into 16 rectangles of 2 different sizes: 8 at 2 × 2.5 × 2.5 cm (¾ × 1 × 1″) and 8 at 1.25 × 2.5 × 0.65 cm (½ × 1 × ¼″). Store in an airtight container and/or freeze for up to 1 week.

LEMON VERBENA-PISTACHIO EMULSION

125 mL (½ cup) lemon juice

25 g (0.9 oz) lemon verbena, coarsely chopped

75 g (2.7 oz) pistachios, shelled

2 large eggs

4 large egg yolks

75 g (2.7 oz) granulated sugar

2.5 g (1¼) gelatin leaves, bloomed

75 g (2.7 oz) unsalted butter

Combine juice and lemon verbena in a microwaveable bowl. Bring to a boil in a microwave oven. Remove from oven, cover tightly with plastic wrap to create a natural vacuum, and allow flavours to infuse for at least 1 hour.

Bring water to a boil in a small saucepan. Blanch pistachios for a few minutes, drain, and place them in the centre of a clean, dry dishtowel. Fold the towel over nuts and rub them lightly to remove skins. Discard skins. Grind nuts in a blender until paste-like. Set aside.

Strain juice and discard lemon verbena. Scald juice in a heavy saucepan. Combine eggs, egg yolks, sugar and pistachio paste in another saucepan; whisk vigorously by hand until the mixture is smooth and creamy.

Pour juice into the egg mixture a little at a time, whisking constantly. Bring the mixture back to a boil, stirring constantly to prevent scorching. Remove from heat and add gelatin. Cool the mixture over an ice-water bath until it reaches body temperature.

Place butter in a food processor. With the motor running, slowly pour in the egg mixture a little at a time so that it emulsifies and thickens. Refrigerate.

Note: Serve cold as a filling or warm as a sauce. For best re-heating results, place emulsion in a microwaveable dish and warm in 15-second intervals. Stir between intervals. Repeat until the mixture is warmed.

DEEP-FRIED RAVIOLI AND PASTA STRANDS

2½ sheets of commercially prepared fresh lasagna

1 L (4 cups) oil for deep-frying

Heat a deep fryer to 180°C (350°F).

Using a rolling pin, roll ½ sheet of lasagna as thin as possible. Cut the dough into thin sticks using a sharp knife. Drop pasta strands in hot oil and fry until golden brown. Remove from oil with a slotted spoon and drain briefly on a paper towel. Cool and store in an airtight container.

Cut 2 sheets of lasagna into 2 × 7.5 cm (¾ × 3″) rectangles. Drop rectangles in hot oil and fry until golden brown. Remove from oil with a slot-

ted spoon and drain briefly on a paper towel. Cool, then cut rectangles in half lengthwise with a paring knife. (The steam trapped in the dough naturally splits the sheets in 2. Run a knife along the edge to open.) Fill the halves with pistachio emulsion to form open-face ravioli.

CHOCOLATE DÉCOR

200 g (7.2 oz) 70% cocoa dark chocolate, tempered

On a sheet of clear acetate or a piece of plastic wrap stretched tight over a board and secured with tape, spread chocolate very thinly with a spatula. Allow it to dry (crystallize). When chocolate is just about hard, cut it into 16 rectangles of 2 different sizes: 8 at 2.5 × 3 cm (1 × 1¼″) and 8 at 2 × 3 (¾ × 1¼″). Store in a cool, dry place, but do not refrigerate.

GARNISH

125 mL (½ cup) Bing cherry reduction, page 153
16 fresh cherries, pitted and quartered
75 g (2.7 oz) pistachios, lightly toasted and finely chopped

ASSEMBLY

Pipe or spoon 2 beads of reduction across each plate, one vertically to the plate and the other on a diagonal. Place a half ravioli over each line of reduction. Top each half ravioli with 4 cherry quarters. Pipe or spoon a bead of emulsion onto the front of the plate and sprinkle with pistachios. Arrange 2 pieces of soft-cake—one of each size—in the empty spaces on the dish. Top each cake with a slightly larger rectangle of chocolate. Sprinkle with pistachios. Garnish with 2 pasta strands placed against one of the ravioli. Serve immediately.

WINE

A Canadian VQA icewine, especially Cabernet Franc, a late-harvest Pinot Gris or even a Tokaji Essencia made with 3 or 4 puttonyos should pair well with the berry and nut flavours of this dessert.

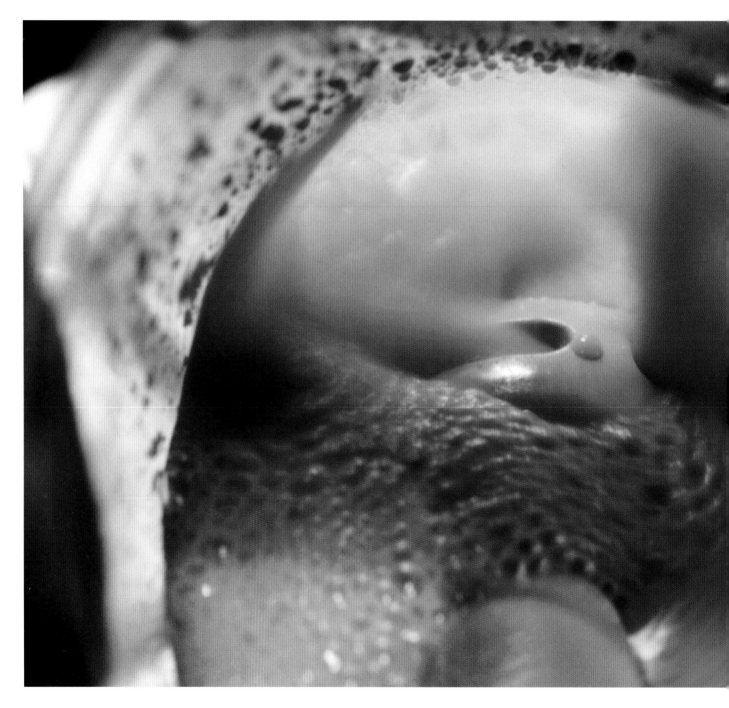

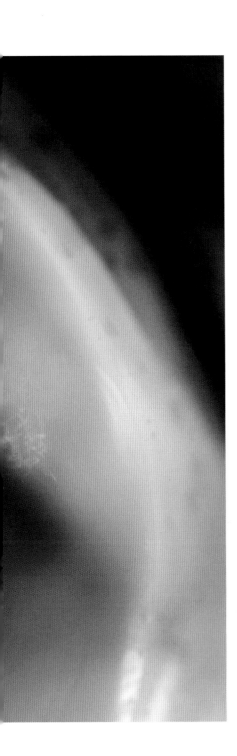

emulsification

Emulsification is the operation of mixing two ingredients that typically do not combine—for example, a fat and a liquid—into a stable, homogeneous mixture that is forced together and held in suspension through the manual or mechanical action of beating, whisking or mixing. Emulsified mixtures are usually thick and satiny in texture. The most common emulsions are savoury mayonnaises and vinaigrettes, but sweet emulsions include fruit juice custards mixed with butter and chocolate ganaches mixed with cream. Regardless of the type of emulsion, separation is the major cause of problems. Here are a few tips to prevent separation:

HERB AND OIL EMULSIONS. Unlike most emulsions which use eggs to stabilize the oils and liquids, these emulsions often depend on a natural emulsifier called xanthan gum, which is available in health food stores. In our recipes, we recommend using pectin to stabilize herb and oil emulsions.

FRUIT AND BUTTER EMULSIONS. Eggs—and their natural emulsifier, lecithin—stabilize fruit and butter emulsions. The secret is simple: the thicker the base mixture, the more stable the end result. We recommend mixing frozen egg yolks with the fruit juice, since frozen yolks are thicker than fresh ones, even when thawed. A thicker base mixture will withstand more agitation and thin out less when emulsified with the butter.

CREAM AND CHOCOLATE EMULSIONS. Cocoa liquor stabilizes the cream (the liquid) and cocoa butter (the fat) in these emulsions. To make a smooth, shiny, elastic and firm ganache, you must have the correct formulation of cocoa butter and cream as well as the right temperature. Watch the amount of sugar in the recipe, as too much added sugar can cause the ganache to separate. As you pour the hot cream over the chopped chocolate, be sure to keep the temperature between 35°C (95°F) and 40°C (105°F) since cocoa butter binds or fuses at 35°C (95°F). If the recipe calls for butter, add it after the ganache is emulsified. Add alcohol after the butter.

Baked blue cheesecake mousse with rhubarb compote and celery confit

———∞∞∞———

CHEESECAKE IS ONE of North America's most popular desserts. Some cheesecakes are rich and dense, others are light and airy; this one is an incredible baked cheesecake uniquely presented as a mousse. Made with subtle yet distinctly flavoured blue cheese, the slight saltiness of the cake is perfect with the sweetness of the rhubarb compote and the celery confit. Rhubarb foam and crunchy tuiles, with their varied textures, round out this dessert. *Serves 8*

BAKED BLUE CHEESECAKE MOUSSE

160 g (5.7 oz) cream cheese
40 g (1.4 oz) blue cheese, such as
    Ermite or Stilton
90 g (3.2 oz) granulated sugar
15 g (0.6 oz) all-purpose flour
250 g (9.1 oz) sour cream
2 large egg yolks
125 g (4.5 oz) cream cheese

Preheat the oven to 150°C (300°F). Line a 12.5 cm (5″) round mould with silicone paper.

Using an electric mixer fitted with a paddle attachment, mix 160 g (5.7 oz) cream cheese, blue cheese and sugar until well combined. Scrape the sides of the bowl with a rubber spatula, and add flour. Mix until thoroughly combined. Add ½ the sour cream and mix again. Scrape the sides of the bowl with the rubber spatula, mixing well to make sure the batter is completely smooth and free of lumps. Stir in remaining sour cream, then egg yolks. Mix until just combined. Pour the batter into the pan and bake for about 35 minutes. Turn the pan and bake for another 10 to 20 minutes, or until light golden brown. Cool. For best results, refrigerate overnight (or at least 3 to 4 hours).

Just before serving, place cheesecake in a food processor. Pulse until cake is broken up. Add 125 g (4.5 oz) cream cheese and pulse until well combined.

RHUBARB COMPOTE

200 g (7.2 oz) fresh or frozen
    rhubarb stalks
10 g (0.4 oz) granulated sugar
6½ mL (1¼ tsp) powdered pectin
100 mL (⅓ cup + 1 Tbsp) rhubarb
    purée, page 151
5 mL (1 tsp) lemon zest
¼ vanilla bean
30 g (1.1 oz) borage honey

If using fresh rhubarb, wash stalks and remove filaments with a paring knife. Cut stalks into large cubes.

In a saucepan, mix sugar and pectin. Add purée and zest. Split vanilla bean in half lengthwise, scrape out seeds, then add seeds and pod to the syrup mixture; bring to a boil. Reduce heat to simmer. Add rhubarb and honey and cook for 10 to 12 minutes, or until fruit is soft but not mushy (the cooking time is substantially less if you use frozen rhubarb). Discard vanilla pod. Serve warm or refrigerate until needed. For best results, reheat refrigerated compote in a microwave oven before serving.

RHUBARB TUILES

50 mL (3 Tbsp + 1 tsp) rhubarb
    purée, page 151
6 g (0.3 oz) black sesame seeds
65 g (2.4 oz) granulated sugar
25 g (0.9 oz) all-purpose flour
25 g (0.9 oz) salted butter, melted

Combine purée, sesame seeds, sugar and flour. Mix well. Fold in butter, and refrigerate the dough, covered, for a couple of hours.

To bake, preheat the oven to 180°C (350°F).

Using the back of a spoon, spread about a teaspoon of dough onto a silicone mat, making a 5 cm (2″) circle. Repeat to make 8 circles. Bake 4 to 6 minutes, or until golden brown and lacy looking. Cool on mat (these tuiles break easily). Store in an airtight container.

Note: The dough can be refrigerated for several days or frozen for several months. For best results, thaw frozen dough in the refrigerator overnight before using.

RHUBARB FOAM

375 mL (1½ cups + 1 Tbsp) rhubarb
    purée, page 151
15 g (0.6 oz) granulated sugar
2 g (1) gelatin leaf, bloomed

Pour purée into a measuring cup. Allow to rest until the sediment settles to the bottom. Pour off clear juice and reserve 125 mL (½ cup). Discard sediment.

Combine juice and sugar in a saucepan; bring to a boil. Remove from heat and add gelatin, stirring well to combine. Pour the liquid into a siphon cream dispenser and add nitrous oxide. Refrigerate until completely cold. Shake well before serving.

continued overleaf

CELERY CONFIT AND CELERY CHIPS

100 g (3.6 oz) celery stalks
150 mL (½ cup + 2 Tbsp) simple
    syrup, page 152

Trim stalks and remove filaments with a paring knife. Using a potato peeler, shave long vertical strips the length of the stalk.

Bring syrup to a boil. Add celery and cook until soft and translucent, about 3 to 5 minutes. Remove from syrup with a slotted spoon. Reserve ½ of celery pieces and refrigerate the rest until serving time. Discard syrup.

Cut reserved celery strips in half and pat dry. Place them on a microwaveable dish and cook on high in 15-second intervals. Turn strips between intervals to dry both sides. As strips begin to dry, cook for shorter and shorter intervals. Store in an airtight container until needed.

GARNISH

8 crystallized celery leaves, page 156
pumpkin seed oil (optional)

ASSEMBLY

Place a tablespoonful of compote in the centre of each dish and top with a tuile. Form a quenelle of mousse and set it in the centre of the tuile. Top with some confit, chips and a leaf. Dispense foam around compote. Using an eye dropper, drizzle oil over foam and compote. Serve immediately.

WINE

A Canadian VQA Cabernet Franc icewine, French Sauternes or Californian port should match wonderfully with the rhubarb and leading cheese flavours of this dessert.

Orange chiboust with nectarine carpaccio and citrus crackers

⊶⊷

A CHIBOUST IS A STIRRED CUSTARD that is lightened with cooked egg whites to produce a cloud-light mixture with a soufflé-like texture. The crunchy fresh vanilla-flavoured nectarine carpaccio adds an incredible burst of freshness to this dish and the remarkably aromatic and surprisingly sweet white balsamic reduction is a wonderful complement for the blood orange. *Serves 8*

ORANGE CHIBOUST

PART I: ORANGE CREAM

50 mL (3 Tbsp + 1 tsp) whipping cream

35 mL (2 Tbsp + 1 tsp) fresh orange juice, page 151

35 mL (2 Tbsp + 1 tsp) thawed orange juice concentrate

zest of 1 orange

20 g (0.7 oz) granulated sugar

10 g (0.4 oz) custard powder

3 large eggs

4 g (2) gelatin leaves, bloomed

Scald cream, juice, concentrate and zest with 10 g (0.35 oz) sugar in a heavy saucepan.

In a bowl, vigorously mix the other 10 g (0.35 oz) sugar with custard powder and eggs, by hand with a whisk, until the mixture is smooth and creamy.

Pour the cream mixture into the egg mixture a little at a time, whisking constantly. Strain this combined mixture back into the saucepan.

Cook the mixture over high heat until it forms bubbles and thickens, stirring constantly with a wire whisk to prevent scorching. Remove from heat, add gelatin and stir well. Keep warm.

PART II

30 mL (2 Tbsp) water

75 g (2.7 oz) granulated sugar

25 g (0.9 oz) corn syrup

2 large egg whites

Line a 15 × 20 × 2 cm (6 × 8 × ¾″) pan with plastic wrap.

Combine water, sugar and syrup in a saucepan; cook over high heat. At the same time, start beating egg whites on low speed using an electric mixer.

When syrup reaches 110°C (230°F), turn the mixer to its highest speed and continue beating egg whites.

When syrup reaches 121°C (250°F), pour it immediately over egg whites while continuing to beat well. Once the mixture is combined, fold this meringue into the orange cream (part 1).

Fill the pan with chiboust. Using a spatula, smooth the top, making it as flat as possible. Refrigerate or place in the freezer until set. Cut into 3.75 cm (1½″) squares and refrigerate until serving time.

NECTARINE CARPACCIO

250 mL (1 cup) simple syrup, page 152

1 fresh vanilla bean, split lengthwise and seeds scraped

2 fresh nectarines

Combine syrup with vanilla seeds. Using a mandoline, slice nectarines as thinly as possible. Soak slices in syrup and refrigerate for a couple hours. Remove nectarines, using a slotted spoon, and transfer to a wire rack to drain.

CITRUS CRACKERS

70 g (2.5 oz) cake flour

35 g (1.2 oz) icing sugar

1 large egg

zest of 1 medium orange

Sift flour and sugar into a bowl. Make a well and add egg and zest, mixing until ingredients are well combined. The dough will be a bit sticky. Wrap the dough in plastic wrap and refrigerate for at least 1 hour.

Place the dough on a lightly floured surface and roll out to a thickness of 2 mm (⅛″). Cut the dough into 8 funky, uneven shapes, at least 3.75 cm (1½″) wide by 10 cm (4″) long. Using 2 or more different-sized cookie cutters or piping tips, make holes in the crackers to give them an airy look.

continued overleaf

Lay each cracker on a piece of aluminum foil. Cut the foil so that the base is exactly the same size as the cracker. (Make sure that the crackers are still formed into funky shapes.) Allow crackers to dry overnight.

To bake, preheat the oven to 180°C (350°F). Bake crackers, still on their foil bases, until lightly golden brown, about 5 minutes. Remove from oven and allow crackers to cool. Remove foil bases. Store in an airtight container.

WHITE BALSAMIC VINEGAR REDUCTION

250 mL (1 cup) white balsamic vinegar

Bring vinegar to a boil in a saucepan. Reduce vinegar to a thick, syrupy consistency. Cool and refrigerate.

CARAMEL POWDER

125 g (4.5 oz) granulated sugar
30 mL (2 Tbsp) water
40 g (1.4 oz) salted butter

Combine sugar and water in a saucepan; cook over high heat until the mixture is caramel in colour. Remove from heat. Decook with butter, mixing until butter is completely incorporated. Pour caramel onto a silicone mat and cool until completely hard.

Break caramel into small shards. In a food processor, grind shards to a fine coffee-like powder.

GARNISH

100 g (3.6 oz) white chocolate, tempered (optional)
2 fresh blood oranges, peeled, seeded and segmented
24 pumpkin seeds, toasted

ASSEMBLY

Place a square of chiboust in the centre of each plate. Top with a few slices of carpaccio. Using a dab of chocolate, glue a cracker behind the chiboust or simply lean a cracker against it. Alternatively, spike a cracker into the chiboust. Arrange 2 segments of orange in front of chiboust and spoon some reduction over them. Sprinkle a line of caramel powder beside the segments and decorate the plate with pumpkin seeds. Serve immediately.

WINE

A Canadian VQA icewine, especially sparkling, or the Essencia made from the very rare orange Muscat, whose characteristics include a spiciness with orange zest overtones, should pair well with the predominant flavours of nectarine and orange and soufflé-like texture of this dessert.

sweet vegetables

The garden

⎯⎯⎯ ⊗⊗⊗ ⎯⎯⎯

VEGETABLES MAY NOT seem like typical ingredients for sweet baked goods, but they can be. Botanically speaking, a vegetable is the edible portion of a herbaceous plant. It includes leaves, roots, tubers, seeds and flowers as well as the fruit of these plants, for example green beans and green peppers. Because they are not sweet it's hard to picture these vegetables making good desserts, but think of such delicious baked goods as carrot cake, zucchini loaf and pumpkin pie.

Not all vegetables are perfect for desserts so it's important to understand the characteristics of each ingredient. Naturally sweet vegetables make the best desserts, but common sense suggests that not every sweet vegetable is a good choice in every situation. For instance, although Vidalia onions are milder tasting than other members of the onion and garlic family—in fact they burst with natural sweetness (especially after cooking)—they are still too strongly flavoured for use in delicate desserts. (We understand that some people enjoy garlic ice cream but we all have to draw a line somewhere!) Root vegetables such as carrots, sweet potatoes, yams, boniato and cassava are milder and they're the perfect foundations for many modern desserts. The two best ways to prepare vegetables for use in desserts are braising and slow-roasting, both of which concentrate and/or caramelize the vegetables' natural sugars.

Try the vegetable-based desserts in this chapter then create variations of your own. Use sweet red peppers instead of tomatoes in the poblano-caramel parfait. Experiment with sweet potatoes instead of squash in the flan. Also, consider using herbs or spices with your vegetables. Pumpkin and cinnamon are, of course, classic in combination. But how about carrot and curry, corn and nutmeg, sweet potato and cloves, or fennel and anise seeds? All it takes is a little imagination.

Red curry squash flan with gnocchi and coconut curry foam

—— ⬤⬤⬤ ——

THIS DESSERT is our modernist version of pumpkin pie—with a spicy twist. The curry in this dish is a sweet blend of cardamom, coriander, cumin, celery seeds, cinnamon and cloves and does not contain any chilies. It adds a wonderfully aromatic spiced sweetness to the delectable warm crispy gnocchi and the delicious buttery soft squash flan. The coconut curry foam perfectly complements the other flavours and the icewine gelée further enriches this dessert. *Serves 8*

RED CURRY SQUASH FLAN

1 medium red curry squash
195 g (6.9 oz) salted butter
130 g (4.6 oz) white chocolate, chopped
3 large eggs
80 g (2.9 oz) granulated sugar

Preheat the oven to 180°C (350°F). Cut squash in half. Remove and discard seeds, then cut each half in half again. Reserve one quarter for garnish. Wrap the remaining three quarters in aluminum foil. Bake until a knife inserted in the skin and flesh penetrates easily, about 30 to 45 minutes. Scrape flesh into a food processor and purée. Discard skins. Reserve 100 g (3.6 oz) purée, storing the rest in an airtight container in the fridge.

Reduce the oven to 150°C (300°F). Line a 15 × 20 cm (6 × 8″) pan with silicone paper.

Melt butter and chocolate in a microwaveable container. In a separate bowl, combine purée, eggs and sugar. Mix well then fold into the chocolate mixture and stir until thoroughly combined. Pour the batter into the pan and bake in a bain-marie for 25 to 30 minutes. Cool then refrigerate before unmoulding. Cut into 2.5 × 6 cm (1 × 2½″) rectangles.

SPICED SQUASH GNOCCHI

125 g (4.5 oz) red curry squash purée (above)
165 g (5.9 oz) all-purpose flour
5 mL (1 tsp) baking powder
60 g (2.1 oz) granulated sugar
pinch of sweet curry powder, or to taste (available at East Indian specialty food stores, or look for a curry powder without chilies)
1 L (4 cups) oil for deep-frying

Heat a deep fryer to 180°C (350°F).

Combine purée, flour and baking powder in a bowl; mix until the dough is soft and does not stick to your fingers. Place the dough on a lightly floured surface and roll out to a thickness of 1.25 cm (½″). Cut the dough into 2.5 cm (1″) squares.

Mix sugar and curry powder in a bowl.

Drop gnocchi in hot oil and fry until golden brown. Remove from oil with a slotted spoon and drop directly into the sugar mixture. Toss to cover completely. Keep warm until serving time.

COCONUT CURRY FOAM

125 mL (½ cup) whipping cream
125 mL (½ cup) coconut milk
2 g (1) gelatin leaf, bloomed
100 g (3.6 oz) white chocolate, melted
3.75 mL (¾ tsp) sweet curry powder
125 mL (½ cup) orange juice, from concentrate
15 g (0.6 oz) egg whites (about ½ large)

Combine cream and coconut milk in a saucepan; bring to a boil. Add gelatin, stirring well to combine.

In a bowl, combine chocolate and curry powder. Pour the milk mixture over the chocolate mixture and mix well. Add juice and stir to combine. Beat in egg whites. Strain, and discard solids. Pour the liquid into a siphon cream dispenser and add nitrous oxide.

CANDIED SQUASH

¼ medium red curry squash, cut into julienne strips
125 mL (½ cup) simple syrup, page 152
75 g (2.7 oz) granulated sugar

Prepare food dehydrator or preheat the oven to 60°C (125°F).

Place strips of squash in a bowl. Pour syrup over top and toss until all strips are well coated.

Pour sugar into a bowl. Toss syrup-coated strips in sugar. Lay strips flat on a silicone mat or paper and bake/dehydrate until dry and crispy, about 40 to 60 minutes. Cool dried squash and store in an airtight container.

GARNISH

80 mL (⅓ cup), VQA Cabernet Franc icewine gelée, page 153, cut into 1.25 cm (½″) squares then halved to make triangles.

ASSEMBLY

Place a flan in the centre of each plate. Top with a few gnocchi and garnish with strips of candied squash. Arrange some pieces of gelée parallel to the flan. Just before serving, dispense some foam on the other side of the flan. Serve immediately.

WINE

A Canadian VQA Cabernet Franc icewine, Tokaji from Hungary or Jurançon from France should pair well with the creamy flavours and vegetable notes of this dessert. A late-harvest Gewürztraminer is another option.

Apple and eggplant croûte with apple butter, cranberry compote and lemon-poached apples

⚬⚬⚬

EGGPLANT BRILLIANTLY COMPLEMENTS the other flavours in this dessert. Its natural creaminess blends magically with the silky smooth textures of almond cream and apple butter. For contrast, the lemon sucrée delivers substance with a perfect crunchy texture while the lemon thyme–apple reduction and cranberry compote add herbal notes and acidity to round off this dessert. The croûte is best served lukewarm. *Serves 8*

APPLE AND EGGPLANT CROÛTE
140 g (5 oz) lemon sucrée dough,
    page 137 (omit mint oil and/or
    replace with lemon thyme oil)
260 g (9.3 oz) almond cream,
    page 155
140 g (5 oz) pastry cream, page 155
1½ medium Golden Delicious apples
4 baby eggplants, unpeeled
15 mL (1 Tbsp) olive oil for spraying
15 mL (1 Tbsp) vanilla sugar or
    granulated sugar

Preheat the oven to 165°C (325°F). Line a 15 × 20 cm (6 × 8") pan with silicone paper.

Roll out dough to a thickness of 2 mm (⅛") and press it into the bottom of the pan. Mix almond and pastry creams and spread them evenly over dough. Peel, core and slice apples to a thickness of 2 mm (⅛"). Slice eggplants to a thickness of 6 mm (⅜"). Alternate rows of apple and eggplant slices until all the cream is covered. Spray or brush fruit with oil. Sprinkle sugar evenly over croûte. Bake 30 minutes. Turn the pan around and bake for another 15 minutes. Cool croûte completely and refrigerate (freeze for best results) before cutting into 2.5 × 5 cm (1 × 2") rectangles.

APPLE BUTTER
2 medium apples
60 mL (¼ cup) Golden Delicious
    apple purée, page 151, or store-
    bought apple juice
55 g (2 oz) granulated sugar
0.625 mL (⅛ tsp) ground cinnamon
pinch of ground cloves

Peel, core and cube apples to a thickness of 2 mm (⅛"). In a saucepan, combine apples, purée, sugar, cinnamon and cloves; cook over low to medium heat until the mixture has the consistency of a thick sauce. Quickly pulse sauce in a food processor or press through a fine-mesh sieve to make sure butter is smooth. Cool and refrigerate.

CRANBERRY COMPOTE
10 g (0.4 oz) granulated sugar
7.5 mL (1½ tsp) powdered pectin
125 mL (½ cup) cranberry purée,
    page 151, or store-bought
    cranberry juice
25 g (0.9 oz) wildflower honey
50 g (1.9 oz) dried cranberries
¼ vanilla bean

In a saucepan, mix sugar and pectin. Add purée, honey and cranberries. Split vanilla bean in half lengthwise, scrape out seeds, then add seeds to the cranberry mixture. Bring to a boil and cook until the mixture is thick and syrupy. Remove from heat and allow to cool. Refrigerate.

LEMON-POACHED APPLES
1 medium Golden Delicious apple
250 mL (1 cup) simple syrup, page 152
juice of 1 fresh lemon

Peel, core and cut apple into 5 mm (¼") dice.

Bring syrup to a boil in a heavy saucepan. Add lemon juice. Cool syrup to body temperature then pour over apples. Soak apples in syrup until just before serving.

LEMON THYME–APPLE REDUCTION
15 g (0.6 oz) granulated sugar
1.25 mL (¼ tsp) powdered pectin
10 g (0.4 oz) wildflower honey
200 mL (¾ cup + 1 Tbsp) apple
    purée, page 151, or store-bought
    apple juice
8 sprigs lemon thyme, or to taste

In a saucepan, mix sugar and pectin. Add honey, purée and lemon thyme. Bring to a boil and cook until the mixture is thick and syrupy. Remove from heat, strain and discard lemon thyme, and allow to cool. Refrigerate.

SPRING ROLL WRAPPER GARNISH
one 20 cm (8") square spring roll
    wrapper
oil for deep-frying

Heat a wok or deep fryer to 180°C (350°F). Cut wrapper in half then into 2.5 cm (1″) rectangles. Using a pair of tongs, fold each rectangle in half. Holding it with the tongs, plunge each rectangle in hot oil and fry lightly. Drain on a paper towel for a few seconds.

GARNISH
8 sprigs lemon thyme

ASSEMBLY
Place a warm croûte in the centre of each plate. Form a quenelle of apple butter and place it on one side. Spoon some compote in front of the croûte. Arrange some cubes of apple on the side opposite the apple butter and drizzle them with reduction. Decorate with spring roll wrapper garnish and a sprig of lemon thyme.

WINE
A Canadian VQA Vidal icewine or French botrytis-affected Chenin Blanc such as Bonnezeaux or Quarts de Chaume should pair well with the almond and apple flavours in this dessert.

Poblano-caramel parfait with fireweed honey-roasted tomatoes and chili matches

TOMATOES, RIPENED TO PERFECTION in the warm summer sun, are plenty sweet and juicy to make incredible desserts. Slow roasted with fireweed honey and fresh lemon, tomatoes bring a tantalizing sweetness and acidity that contrasts the frozen parfait and crispy chili matches. Each mouthful is a truly unique experience: the delicate heat of the chilies becomes noticeable only after the buttery soft tomatoes are swallowed and the coolness of the parfait dissipates. *Serves 8*

POBLANO-CARAMEL PARFAIT

125 g (4.5 oz) granulated sugar

30 mL (2 Tbsp) water

1 dried poblano chili pepper, finely chopped *or* 2.5 mL (½ tsp) chili powder, or to taste

40 g (1.4 oz) salted butter

3 large egg yolks

1 large egg

30 mL (2 Tbsp) water

160 mL (⅔ cup) whipped cream (in soft peaks)

Combine sugar, 30 mL (2 Tbsp) water and chili in a saucepan; cook over high heat until the mixture is caramel in colour. Remove from heat. Decook with butter, mixing until butter is completely incorporated. Pour caramel onto a silicone mat and cool until completely hard.

Break caramel into small shards. In a food processor, grind the shards to a fine coffee-like powder. Reserve 75 g (2.7 oz) and store the rest in an airtight container.

Combine egg yolks, egg, 30 mL (2 Tbsp) water and caramel powder in a stainless steel bowl. Place the bowl over a saucepan of simmering but not boiling water on medium heat, and whisk until the mixture reaches 85°C (185°F), or until the mixture is foamy. Remove from heat and cool to room temperature.

Using a rubber spatula, gently fold cream into the caramel mixture. Pour into 5 cm (2″) round or oval flexible silicone moulds or metal ring moulds lined with a strip of silicone paper. Freeze.

CRISPY CHILI MATCHES

PART I: PRE-FERMENTED DOUGH

4 g (0.2 oz) dried yeast

30 mL (2 Tbsp) warm water

40 g (1.4 oz) all-purpose flour

Dissolve yeast in warm water, stirring constantly until yeast is completely dissolved. Add flour and mix by hand until the dough forms a shiny ball. Place dough in a lightly oiled stainless steel or glass bowl, cover tightly with plastic wrap, and refrigerate overnight.

PART II

4 g (0.2 oz) dried yeast

30 mL (2 Tbsp) warm whole milk

80 g (2.9 oz) all-purpose flour

2.5 mL (½ tsp) chili powder

15 g (0.6 oz) granulated sugar

1½ large egg yolks

15 g (0.6 oz) salted butter

500 mL (2 cups) oil for deep-frying

In the bowl of an electric mixer fitted with a dough hook, dissolve yeast in warm milk, stirring constantly until yeast is completely dissolved. Add flour, chili powder, sugar, egg yolks and butter, and mix on low speed until the dough forms a smooth and shiny ball. Add pre-fermented dough and continue mixing until thoroughly combined. Cover dough with a tea towel, set in a warm place away from drafts, and allow dough to rest until it doubles in size, about 1 hour.

Punch down the dough with your fists and, using a rolling pin, roll it out to a thickness of about 2 mm (⅛″). Transfer the sheet of dough to a cutting board and place in the freezer until dough is completely frozen.

To cook, preheat a deep fryer to 180°C (350°F). Remove dough from freezer and cut in julienne strips. Drop strips in hot oil, allowing them to form funky shapes, and fry until golden brown. Remove from oil with a slotted spoon and drain briefly on a paper towel. Keep at room temperature until serving time.

FIREWEED HONEY-ROASTED TOMATOES AND COMPOTE

8 Roma tomatoes, halved and seeded

juice of 3 fresh lemons

60 g (2.1 oz) salted butter, melted

125 mL (½ cup) olive oil

150 g (5.3 oz) granulated sugar

20 g (0.7 oz) fireweed honey

90 g (3.2 oz) dried fruit (cranberries, cherries, blueberries, apricots)

continued overleaf

Preheat the oven to 180° C (350° F). Arrange tomatoes cut-side down in a 25 cm (10″) square pan, ensuring that halves are close together but not overlapping.

In a bowl, combine juice, butter, oil, sugar and honey. Mix well and pour over tomatoes. Cover the pan tightly with aluminum foil and bake until skins are wrinkled, about 35 minutes. Remove foil and bake for another 10 minutes to brown the tomatoes. Remove tomatoes with a slotted spoon, reserving cooking juice, and keep warm until serving time.

Strain cooking juice into a saucepan over high heat and discard solids. Reduce cooking juice to half. Stir in dried fruit, reduce heat to medium, and allow sauce to simmer until the mixture is thick and syrupy. Keep the compote warm until serving time or refrigerate in a plastic container until needed.

GARNISH

30 g (1.1 oz) sunflower seeds, toasted
5 mL (1 tsp) granulated sugar, mixed
  with 5 mL (1 tsp) chili powder

ASSEMBLY

Place a frozen parfait slightly off centre on each plate. Place 2 warm tomato halves in front of it. Spoon some compote over tomatoes and sprinkle with sunflower seeds. Top parfait with a few chili matches and sprinkle everything with a bit of chili sugar. Serve immediately.

WINE

A Canadian VQA Gewürztraminer icewine or Austrian Trockenbeerenauslese (Welschriesling and Chardonnay blend) should pair well with the citrus, caramel and spice notes of this dessert.

Carrot cake with peach-ginger cream and Saskatoon berry compote

⠿

CARROTS ARE WIDELY USED in desserts in North America. Their natural sweetness is the perfect match for the spiciness of the ginger and the bitterness of the citrus reduction, which almost magically becomes sweet again with a sprinkle of fleur de sel. The freshness of the peach and the almost perfume-like intensity of the berry make this carrot cake truly original. *Serves 8*

CARROT CAKE

2 large eggs
235 g (8.5 oz) granulated sugar
125 mL (½ cup) vegetable oil
160 g (5.7 oz) carrots, grated
165 g (5.9 oz) all-purpose flour
5 mL (1 tsp) ground cinnamon
5 mL (1 tsp) baking soda
5 mL (1 tsp) baking powder
35 g (1.2 oz) walnut pieces
70 g (2.5 oz) raisins

Preheat the oven to 165°C (325°F). Line a 15 × 20 cm (6 × 8″) pan with silicone paper.

Mix eggs and sugar in a large bowl. Add oil and then carrots and combine.

In another bowl, sift together flour, cinnamon, baking soda and baking powder. Add dry ingredients to wet and mix until thoroughly combined. Fold in walnuts and raisins. Pour the batter into the pan and bake for 35 to 45 minutes. Unmould the cake and allow it to cool on a wire rack.

For best results, freeze the cake before cutting it into 4 × 6.5 cm (1½ × 2½″) rectangles. Wrap each well in plastic wrap and freeze them in an airtight container until ready to use. Thaw and refrigerate before serving. The cake will keep frozen up to 1 month.

PEACH-GINGER CREAM

125 mL (½ cup) whole milk
125 mL (½ cup) peach purée, page 151
30 g (1.1 oz) granulated sugar
5 mL (1 tsp) fresh grated ginger
30 g (1.1 oz) granulated sugar
25 g (0.9 oz) custard powder
1 large egg

Scald milk, purée, 30 g (1.1 oz) sugar and ginger in a heavy saucepan.

In a bowl, vigorously mix another 30 g (1.1 oz) sugar with custard powder and egg, by hand with a whisk, until the mixture is smooth and creamy.

Pour the milk mixture into the egg mixture a little at a time, whisking constantly. Strain this combined mixture back into the saucepan. Discard ginger.

Cook the mixture over high heat until it forms bubbles and thickens, stirring constantly with a wire whisk to prevent scorching. Remove from heat, transfer to a clean container, and cover immediately with plastic wrap pressed right against the cream. Using the sharp point of a knife, puncture about 6 holes to allow steam to escape. Cool and refrigerate. The cream will keep refrigerated for 3 to 4 days.

SASKATOON BERRY COMPOTE

10 g (0.4 oz) granulated sugar
7.5 mL (1½ tsp) powdered pectin
25 g (0.9 oz) fireweed honey
125 mL (½ cup) port
50 g (1.9 oz) dried Saskatoon berries or dried blueberries
¼ vanilla bean

In a saucepan, mix sugar and pectin. Add honey, port and berries. Split vanilla bean in half lengthwise, scrape out seeds, then add seeds to the berry mixture. Discard pod. Heat slowly until berries absorb liquid and swell to about twice their original size. Cook until the mixture is thick and syrupy. Keep at room temperature until serving time, or refrigerate for up to 1 week.

PEACH CHIPS

15 mL (1 Tbsp) olive oil
½ fresh peach, peeled

Spread a very thin layer of oil on a microwaveable dinner plate. Cut peach into paper-thin slices and spread them on the plate. Place slices so that they don't touch. Dry slices in a microwave oven in 15-second intervals on high. Turn slices between intervals to dry both sides. As slices begin to dry, cook for shorter and shorter intervals so that natural sugars do not caramelize.

Repeat until all moisture has evaporated. Cool chips on a paper towel or a wire rack. *Yield: About 24 slices*

GARNISH

8 scoops peach sorbet, page 155
8 buckwheat honey gingersnaps, page 134, rolled into 2 mm (⅛″) thick and 4.5 cm (1¾″) in diameter rounds
16 buckwheat honey gingersnaps, page (59), rolled into 2 mm (⅛″) thick and 7.5 × 0.5 cm (3 × ¼″) long sticks

1 fresh peach, cut into wedges
125 mL (½ cup) citrus reduction, page 153
10 mL (2 tsp) fleur de sel

ASSEMBLY

Place a piece of cake in the centre of each plate. Pipe two beads of cream on top and arrange compote beside the cream. Scoop a ball of sorbet onto a round gingersnap. Place cookie beside cake and spike

2 gingersnap sticks into sorbet. Arrange peach wedges on opposite side of cake. Spoon reduction over wedges, sprinkle with fleur de sel, and top with a peach chip.

WINE

A Canadian VQA Gewürztraminer icewine or Sélection de Grains Nobles Gewürztraminer from the French Alsace should pair well with the spice notes of ginger and cinnamon in this dessert.

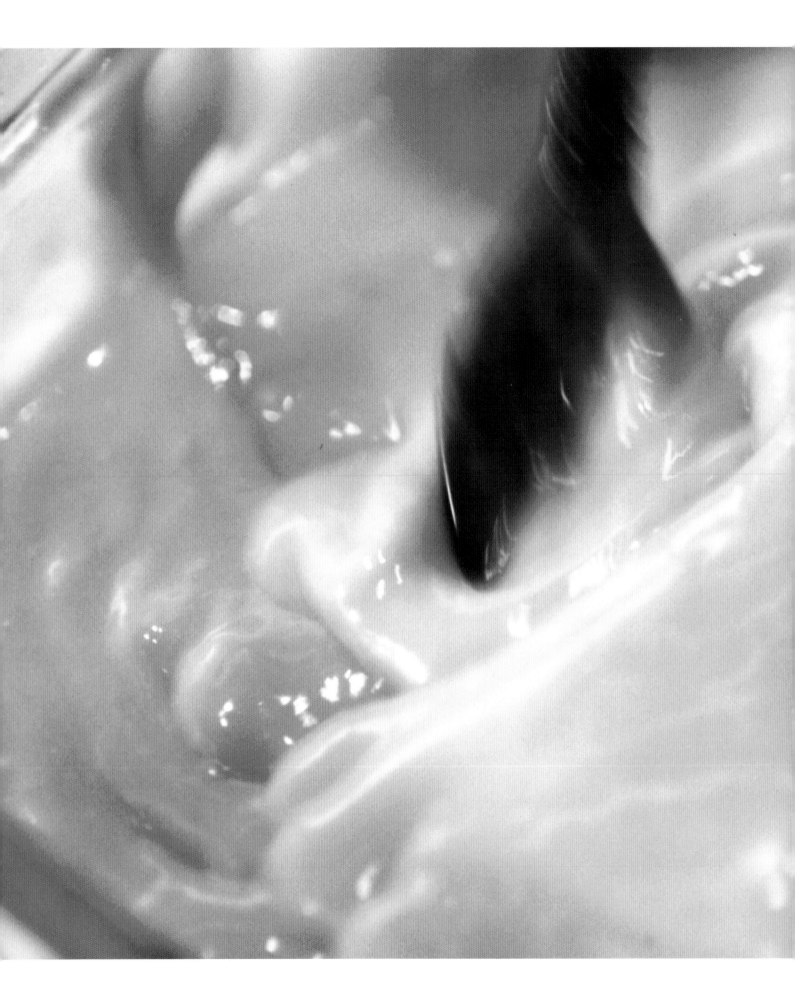

Gelatinization

Gelatinization is the operation of thickening a preparation, such as custard or sauce, using a starch. (Note that coagulated custards are referred to as "baked" whereas gelatinized custards are referred to as "stirred.") Although starches look like fine powdered solids, they are actually granules that are insoluble in cold water. In heated water, however, the granules soften, start to absorb water and then swell and rupture. As the starch leaches into the water, the liquid thickens to become a translucent mixture, a gel. Gelatinization typically starts at 77°C (170°F) and is complete at the boiling point. Here are a few tips to keep in mind to ensure successful gelatinization:

STARCHES. Starches are either amyloses (grain origin) or amylopectins (root or tuber origin). The most effective starch for gelatinization is an amylose, such as wheat or corn starch, because it thickens just below the boiling point and can be held at that temperature without damage. It also sets to a firm gel and can be reheated without breaking, but it does not freeze successfully. For a dessert that will be frozen, select an amylopectin, such as arrowroot, which will freeze without damage.

ACIDS AND SUGARS. Adding an acid, such as lemon juice, or too much sugar will inhibit the gelatinization process. If the dessert needs acid or more sugar, let the product gel completely before adding the acid and/or more sugar.

ENZYMES. Raw egg yolks contain an enzyme called alpha-amylase that causes custards to separate after gelatinization. The enzyme attacks the starch that sets the custard, typically within the first 12 hours, and liquid separates from the custard and settles as a pool at the bottom of the bowl. To prevent this separation, destroy the enzyme by cooking the custard as close to the boiling point as possible for 1 minute once gelatinization starts.

Pan-fried bread pudding with orange-braised chicon and chicory ice cream

⟨⟨⟨⟨⟩⟩⟩⟩

BELGIAN ENDIVE, OR CHICON as it is called in Belgium, is commonly cooked with sugar, even in savoury dishes. On a visit to see family in Belgium, we came across a Michelin 3-star restaurant that served chicon as a dessert. Since then we've created our own version that marries the unexpected, somewhat hauntingly bittersweet flavour of the chicon with a creamy soft and warm bread pudding. Cool chicory ice cream, with its coffee-like flavour, rounds out the dish. *Serves 8*

PAN-FRIED BREAD PUDDING

1 apple, peeled, cored and cut in
    5 mm (¼″) dice
30 mL (2 Tbsp) fruit stock, page 151
250 mL (1 cup) whole milk
60 g (2.1 oz) granulated sugar
2 large eggs
1.25 mL (¼ tsp) ground cinnamon
125 g (4.5 oz) bread, cut in 2.5 cm (1″)
    dice (day-old crusty French bread
    is best)
25 g (0.9 oz) 70% cocoa dark choco-
    late, finely chopped
15 g (0.6 oz) salted butter

Preheat the oven to 150°C (300°F). Line a 15 × 20 cm (6 × 8″) pan with silicone paper.

Combine apple and stock in a small saucepan over high heat; cover and steam briefly until apple pieces release their juice, about 2 to 3 minutes. Remove the lid and pan-fry until all liquid has evaporated. Apple dice must remain whole and not mushy. Cool.

Whisk milk, sugar, eggs and cinnamon in a small bowl. Pour this mixture over bread cubes. Allow to stand 5 minutes.

Sift chocolate through a fine-mesh sieve to remove powder. Discard powder. Stir chocolate and apples into the soaked bread mixture. Pour into the pan and bake in a bain-marie in the oven for about 25 minutes. We recommend that you place a piece of silicone paper on top of pudding while baking to prevent it from drying out.

Allow pudding to cool, then unmould and refrigerate overnight.

Cut pudding into 4 × 4 cm (1½″ × 1½″) squares. Heat butter in a frying pan and pan-fry squares until light brown on both sides. Keep warm until serving time.

ORANGE-BRAISED CHICON

4 chicons (Belgian endives)
8 sugar cubes
40 g (1.4 oz) salted butter
juice of 2 oranges
lemon juice, to taste

Cut chicons in half lengthwise. Combine chicons, sugar, butter and juices in a saucepan. Cook, covered, over low heat for about 20 minutes, or until a knife inserted in the chicon flesh penetrates easily. Cut each chicon in half lengthwise. Reserve 30 mL (2 Tbsp) cooking juice for the caramel sauce. Keep warm until serving.

CHICORY ICE CREAM

250 mL (1 cup) whole milk
75 mL (¼ cup + 1 Tbsp) whipping
    cream
5 mL (1 tsp) chicory
30 g (1.1 oz) granulated sugar
0.625 mL (⅛ tsp) powdered pectin
3 large egg yolks
200 mL (¾ cup + 1 Tbsp) whole milk

Pour 250 mL (1 cup) milk and cream into a saucepan; bring to a boil. Add chicory, remove from heat, cover tightly with plastic wrap to create a natural vacuum, and allow flavours to infuse for at least 15 minutes.

In a stainless steel bowl, combine sugar and pectin. Add egg yolks; whisk lightly until well mixed. Set aside.

Place 200 mL (¾ cup + 1 Tbsp) milk in a saucepan; bring to a boil. Add to chicory infusion. Strain and discard chicory. Pour the milk mixture into the egg mixture a little at a time, whisking constantly. Place the bowl over a saucepan of simmering but not boiling water on medium heat, and whisk until the mixture reaches 85°C (185°F), or until the mixture coats the back of a spoon. Cool. Transfer to a clean container with a lid and refrigerate overnight. Churn using an ice cream machine.

CARAMEL SAUCE

90 g (3.2 oz) granulated sugar
20 g (0.7 oz) corn syrup
30 mL (2 Tbsp) water
60 mL (¼ cup) whipping cream
75 g (2.7 oz) maple syrup
25 g (0.9 oz) salted butter
30 mL (2 Tbsp) chicon cooking
    juice (above)

Combine sugar, corn syrup and water in a saucepan; cook over high heat until the mixture is caramel in colour. Remove from heat.

Combine cream, maple syrup, butter and cooking juice in a bowl. Pour into caramel to decook. Refrigerate.

GARNISH

100 g (3.6 oz) hot caramel, page 156, drizzled onto a silicone mat and formed into eight 5 cm (2″) round lacy décors

ASSEMBLY

Spoon some sauce in the centre of each plate. Curl 2 pieces of warm chicon into a circle and place it over the sauce. Place a piece of warm pudding on top of chicon. Decorate with a disk of caramel lace and a scoop or quenelle of ice cream.

WINE

A Canadian vQA Pinot Blanc ice-wine or French Semillon/Sauvignon Blanc, such as Sauternes (or Sauternes-style) or Barsac, should pair well with the butterscotch/caramel and orange flavours in this dessert. A Vin Santo is another option.

chocolate

The leading ingredient

———⊗⊗⊗———

CHOCOLATE, AS WE KNOW IT, began as a bitter treat of raw, pounded cocoa beans that the Aztecs chewed with a little water. How far chocolate has come since then! To make chocolate today, cocoa beans are removed from their pods, then fermented, dried, roasted and cracked to separate the nibs from the shells. Grinding the nibs extracts cocoa butter and produces a thick, dark paste called chocolate liquor. When refined, and with sugar and milk added, this liquor is ready for conching. Huge machines with rotating blades slowly blend the heated chocolate liquor to remove residual moisture and acids, and as the machines work their magic, they turn a largely bitter liquid into pure smooth chocolate.

Today chocolate, or couverture as it's called commercially, is a connoisseur food. With so many varieties to choose from, it's hard to know what to buy. In our experience, the single most important factor in determining success with chocolate is its quality. The quality and quantity of the raw and added ingredients, and the way they are incorporated play a very big role in the quality of the final product. For example, too much fat results in a less-intense and cloying chocolate whereas too much sugar inhibits the chocolate flavour.

The type of beans largely determines the flavour—select Criolla beans, for example, impart a deep and pure cocoa flavour. The conching time affects the texture; an extended conching period will result in a smoother chocolate with greater melting properties. Even if you have a recipe for the most delicious chocolate cake, if it is made with an inferior chocolate, the cake will never deliver its full sensory potential.

Working with chocolate offers many opportunities to create unforgettable tastes and textures. To get the best results, you should understand the factors that define quality and that differentiate one type of chocolate from another.

THE LOOK

Look for signs of freshness. Check the expiry date and buy only what you can consume within 2 weeks. Look for signs of fat bloom—pale grey streaks and blotches on the surface of the chocolate, which indicate that it has been exposed to overly warm temperatures (including sunlight near a window, a hot lamp) and that the cocoa butter is rising to the surface. Look too for signs of sugar bloom—grey sugar crystals forming on the surface of the chocolate, which indicate that it has been exposed to dampness (do not store chocolate in the fridge). The chocolate should be shiny and without blemishes and it should break cleanly without crumbling.

THE SMELL

A well-rounded aroma is what you want. Chocolate easily picks up odours from products it is stored near (from laundry soap to onions), so keep unused portions of chocolate well wrapped and in an airtight container, and away from strong odours.

THE SOUND

Listen for a loud, crisp break when you bite into a piece of chocolate.

THE TASTE

The chocolate should melt easily in your mouth without clinging to your palate. It should be smooth and creamy on the tongue and release the distinctive notes and flavours associated with the chocolate you are eating.

UNSWEETENED, BITTER OR BAKING CHOCOLATE

Typically contains no sugar and is used for baking. This type of chocolate is not included in this book as we prefer to use cocoa powder if we want to increase the chocolate/cocoa flavour in a dessert or in other sweet preparations such as sorbets and cake mixes.

DARK CHOCOLATE

Sold interchangeably as bittersweet or semi-sweet chocolate, depending on the amount of sugar added by the manufacturer. It contains anywhere from 35% to 99% combined cocoa solids (liquor and butter). The higher the percentage, the more bitter the chocolate. Typically, this type of chocolate is used for fillings, mousses, custards, soft-texture/soufflé-like cakes, etc. The best flavour pairings include cinnamon, coffee, nuts (especially almonds and pecans) and fruit such as dark cherries and bananas. You should look for a chocolate that has a good balance of strong cocoa notes with just enough sugar; it should be more bitter than sweet. Select a 70% cocoa dark chocolate with a deep and intense bitter cocoa flavour, light acidic notes and a long-lasting intensity in the mouth.

MILK CHOCOLATE

This type of chocolate is the most popular in North America and should contain at least 12% milk solids. Typically, it is used for fillings, mousses, custards, parfaits, etc. The best flavour pairings include caramel, citrus oils (zest), nuts (especially hazelnuts), orange liqueurs like Grand Marnier or Cointreau and fruit such as passion fruit and oranges. You should look for a chocolate that has a good balance— not too sweet but with noticeable cocoa and dairy notes—and that melts easily. Select a milk chocolate with caramel and full cream flavours and a creamy and smooth feel in the mouth.

WHITE CHOCOLATE

Contains no cocoa liquor, just cocoa butter, and is therefore not technically a chocolate product. As white chocolate contains a lot of milk solids, look for a chocolate that is cream/ivory in colour, which means that it contains a higher percentage of cocoa butter. Typically, this type of chocolate is used for fillings, mousses, custards, soft-texture cakes, etc. and as an alternative sweetener. The best flavour pairings include cinnamon, sesame oil, coconut, rum and fruit such as red berries, especially raspberries. You should look for a chocolate that has characteristics similar to milk chocolate and that is definitely not too sweet or thick. Select a white chocolate with distinct fresh milk and butter flavours and a smooth and creamy texture.

Note: All the recipes in this section have been made and tested using fine dark chocolate with a cocoa content of 70%. Using a higher or lower percentage will affect binding properties. That is, other percentages may set differently, thereby significantly changing the consistency of the dessert. When choosing milk or white chocolate, select a premium brand to ensure best results.

Baked chocolate mousse with
mandarin oranges and anise seed croustillant

⎯⎯⎯⎯◦◦◦◦⎯⎯⎯⎯

THIS SURPRISING VERSION of a chocolate mousse is as sensually satisfying as the unbaked original. For an even creamier texture, reduce or omit the dark chocolate and serve the softer mousse in a glass. Mandarin oranges add a special twist to the classic chocolate and orange combination. If mandarins are unavailable, navel oranges are a fine substitute in both the mousse and the sorbet. *Serves 8*

BAKED CHOCOLATE MOUSSE

35 g (1.2 oz) milk chocolate, finely chopped

60 g (2.1 oz) 70% cocoa dark chocolate, finely chopped

5 mL (1 tsp) mandarin napoleon liqueur

10 mL (2 tsp) mandarin orange juice, page 151

1 large egg

1 large egg yolk

15 g (0.6 oz) granulated sugar

45 mL (3 Tbsp) whipping cream

Preheat the oven to 150°C (300°F). Line a shallow 15 cm (6″) square pan with silicone paper.

Combine chocolates, liqueur and juice in a stainless steel bowl. Place the bowl over a saucepan of simmering but not boiling water on medium heat, and stir until all ingredients are melted and the mixture is smooth. Remove from heat and set aside.

Using an electric mixer fitted with a whisk, foam the egg, egg yolk and sugar on the highest speed until the mixture is light yellow in colour and no longer gains volume (about 5 minutes).

In another bowl, whip cream until it forms soft peaks.

Using a rubber spatula, fold ½ of the chocolate into the egg mixture. Combine. Fold in the remaining ½ of the chocolate and combine well. Once thoroughly combined, fold in the cream. Pour this mousse mixture into the pan and cover with aluminum foil. Punch a few holes in the foil to allow steam to escape, and bake the mousse in a bain-marie for about 15 minutes. Rotate the pan so the mousse cooks evenly and bake for another 15 minutes. Remove from the oven and cool.

For best cutting results, allow the mousse to set in the freezer overnight. Cut frozen mousse into 7.5 × 2 cm (3 × ¾″) pieces and allow to thaw in the fridge.

GARNISH

1 recipe chocolate gelée, page 153

3 mandarin oranges, peeled and segmented

75 mL (¼ cup + 1 Tbsp) mandarin reduction, page 153

8 scoops mandarin orange sorbet, page 155

16 anise seed and almond croustillants, page 156, cut into 2.5 cm (1″) circles before baking (for best results, bake in silicone moulds so they keep their exact shape and size)

ASSEMBLY

Liquefy a third of the gelée by putting it in a microwave oven for a few seconds on high. Spoon a bead of gelée onto the centre of each dish. Arrange 3 segments of orange over the gelée and drizzle some reduction on either side of them. Place a slice of mousse on top of the oranges. Top with a scoop of sorbet sandwiched between 2 disks of croustillant. Serve immediately.

WINE

The effervescence of Moscato d'Asti or California orange Muscat will present a spiciness with orange zest overtones that should complement the light texture of the baked mousse and the flavour of the mandarin oranges.

White chocolate and rice milk flan with pistachio emulsion

—∞∞∞—

TWO CULINARY CULTURES meet in this extraordinary dessert. From Europe comes the pairing of the time-honoured flan with a modern emulsion, and from Asia comes the minimalist approach to presentation. As well, the leading flavours of Europe—chocolate and pistachio—meet the leading flavours of Asia—rice and ginger—to create a dish that is stunning. *Serves 8*

WHITE CHOCOLATE AND RICE MILK FLAN

175 mL (⅔ cup + 1 Tbsp) whipping cream
20 g (0.7 oz) lemon grass, chopped
25 g (0.9 oz) granulated sugar
5 g (2 ½) gelatin leaves, bloomed
60 g (2.1 oz) white chocolate
200 mL (¾ cup + 1 Tbsp) rice milk

Combine cream and lemon grass in a saucepan; bring to a boil. Remove from heat, cover tightly with plastic wrap to create a natural vacuum, and allow flavours to infuse for at least 30 minutes.

Strain cream into a measuring cup and discard lemon grass. Make sure that you have 135 mL (½ cup + 1 Tbsp) of cream; top up with regular whipping cream if necessary. Scald cream with sugar in a saucepan, stirring constantly to prevent scorching. Remove from heat and add gelatin and chocolate, stirring well to combine. Add milk and mix until well combined.

Pour the batter into flexible silicone moulds or ramekins. Cover and refrigerate until set, about 4 hours.

RICE PAPER SALAD

500 mL (2 cups) water
300 g (10.8 oz) granulated sugar
60 g (2.1 oz) fresh ginger, grated

six 30 cm (12″) diameter sheets rice paper
20 g (0.7 oz) pistachios, shelled and finely chopped

Combine water, sugar and ginger in a saucepan; bring to a boil. Remove from heat, cover tightly with plastic wrap to create a natural vacuum, and allow flavours to infuse for at least 20 minutes.

Strain syrup into a large flat container and discard ginger. Allow syrup to cool to body temperature.

To bake, preheat the oven to 180°C (350°F). Rehydrate rice paper in syrup for about 15 minutes. Place paper on a cutting board and cut 2 sheets into 3.75 cm (1½″) diameter rounds (about 24 rounds). Cut the other 4 sheets into julienne strips. Place the circles on a silicone mat and sprinkle them with pistachios. Spread ½ the julienne on the same mat and bake for about 7 minutes. Cool.

Store baked paper in an airtight container in a cool dry place. Place remaining unbaked julienne in an airtight container and refrigerate.

PISTACHIO EMULSION

50 g (1.9 oz) pistachios, shelled
160 mL (⅔ cup) whipping cream
½ lemon grass stalk
zest of 1 lime
10 g (0.4 oz) granulated sugar
50 mL (3 Tbsp + 1 tsp) mineral water

1 g (½) gelatin leaf, bloomed
125 g (4.5 oz) white chocolate, finely chopped
5 mL (1 tsp) pistachio oil

Blanch pistachios in a small saucepan for a few minutes, drain, and place them in the centre of a clean, dry dishtowel. Fold the towel over nuts and rub them lightly to remove skins. Discard skins. Set nuts aside.

Combine cream, lemon grass and zest in a saucepan; bring to a boil. Remove from heat, cover tightly with plastic wrap to create a natural vacuum, and allow flavours to infuse for at least 30 minutes.

Strain cream into a measuring cup and discard lemon grass and zest. Make sure that you have 125 mL (½ cup) of cream; top up with regular whipping cream if necessary. Return cream to saucepan, add sugar and water, and bring back to the boil, stirring constantly to prevent scorching. Remove from heat and add gelatin, stirring well to combine.

Place chocolate in a medium bowl. Pour hot cream over chocolate and mix well. Pour the mixture into a food processor or high-speed blender. With the motor running,

add pistachios and oil, and pulse until nuts are finely ground and the mixture is smooth and creamy. Refrigerate.

If the mixture separates, re-emulsify just before serving using a food processor or a high-speed blender.

ASSEMBLY

Place a flan in the centre of each plate. Drizzle some emulsion around the flan. Arrange 3 rice paper circles on top and decorate with baked julienne strips. Garnish with a bunch of unbaked julienne strips, placed on top of the baked ones. Serve immediately.

WINE

A Canadian VQA late-harvest or icewine Gewürztraminer, botrytised or icewine Riesling should pair well with the ginger, nut and creamy flavours of this dessert.

Chocolate custard cake with exotic fruit gelée and caramelized bananas

—⊗—

THIS CAKE has an incredibly intense chocolate flavour and a texture that's as smooth as silk. It is perfect paired with banana, and the slightly acid exotic fruit gelée and cloud-light foam raise this dessert to gustatory ecstasy. *Serves 6 to 8.*

CHOCOLATE CUSTARD CAKE

200 g (7.2 oz) salted butter
130 g (4.6 oz) 70% cocoa dark chocolate, chopped
100 g (3.6 oz) banana purée, page 151
3 large eggs
80 g (2.9 oz) granulated sugar

Preheat oven to 150°C (300°F). Line a 15 × 20 cm (6 × 8″) pan with silicone paper.

Melt butter and chocolate in a microwaveable container.

In a separate bowl, combine purée, eggs and sugar. Add to the chocolate mixture, and mix until thoroughly combined. Pour the batter into the pan and bake in a bain-marie for 25 to 30 minutes. Cool in the fridge before unmoulding. Cut into 6.25 cm (2½″) squares. Cut each square in half on the diagonal to make 2 triangles.

EXOTIC FRUIT FOAM

125 mL (½ cup) whipping cream
50 g (1.9 oz) white chocolate, chopped
60 mL (¼ cup) exotic fruit purée, page 151
15 g (0.6 oz) egg whites (about ½ large)

Bring cream to a boil in a saucepan. Place chocolate in a bowl; pour cream over chocolate, stirring with a rubber spatula until all solids are dissolved. Mix in purée and egg whites. Strain, and discard solids. Pour the liquid into a siphon cream dispenser and add nitrous oxide. Refrigerate.

CHOCOLATE STICKS

55 g (2 oz) icing sugar
45 g (1.6 oz) all-purpose flour
10 g (0.4 oz) unsweetened cocoa powder
55 g (2 oz) salted butter, softened
45 g (1.6 oz) egg whites (about 1½ large)

Sift sugar, flour and cocoa into a large bowl. Using a rubber spatula, incorporate butter and egg whites. Refrigerate until set, about 1 hour.

To bake, preheat the oven to 180°C (350°F). Spread a thin even layer of dough onto a silicone mat. Using a decorating comb with square ends (cut pointed tips out of a regular decorating comb to make ends square), draw parallel lines 7.5 cm (3″) long and 2 mm (⅛″) wide. Bake for 4 to 6 minutes. Cool and store in an airtight container for up to 1 week.

Note: A silicone mat works better than silicone paper, which wrinkles when humid.

CARAMELIZED BANANAS

1 banana
30 g (1.1 oz) granulated sugar

Peel and slice banana into 3.75 cm (1½″) pieces, cut on the diagonal. Sprinkle with sugar and quickly caramelize on one side in a hot nonstick pan. Serve immediately.

GARNISH

80 mL (⅓ cup) exotic fruit gelée, page 153, frozen in a shallow pan to a depth of 2 mm (⅛″) and cut into 0.5 × 1.5 cm (¼ × ¾″) rectangles

ASSEMBLY

Place a triangle of cake in the centre of each plate. Arrange pieces of gelée around the cake. Dispense foam into a cup. Roughly form a quenelle of foam with a soup spoon and place in front of the cake. Decorate with 2 banana slices and 4 chocolate sticks.

WINE

A Portuguese late-bottled vintage (LBV) port, California style port or a French Muscat Beaumes-de-Venise should work well with the leading chocolate flavour and the lightness of the foam. A tawny port or even a Madeira should also suit.

Creamy white chocolate and cranberry risotto with roasted apricots

THIS DESSERT is comfort food at its best. We've taken a basic rice pudding and given it risotto influences, but instead of the traditional arborio rice we use short-grain rice for a less starchy texture. White chocolate makes this dessert creamier still. For a variation, try apples and raisins in place of the apricots and cranberries. *Serves 6*

WHITE CHOCOLATE AND CRANBERRY RISOTTO

220 g (7.9 oz) short-grain rice
15 mL (1 Tbsp) almond or peanut oil
4 mL (¾ tsp) fresh ginger, finely grated
370 mL (1½ cup + 2 tsp) fruit stock, page 151
90 mL (⅓ cup + 2 tsp) whipping cream
45 g (1.6 oz) white chocolate, melted
40 g (1.4 oz) dried apricots, finely chopped
40 g (1.4 oz) dried cranberries, finely chopped

Wash rice in a strainer or colander. Rinse well with cold water until the rinse water runs clear.

Heat oil in a saucepan over medium heat. Add rice, stirring well to make sure that all grains are coated. Add ginger and cover with stock. Bring the rice mixture to a boil then reduce heat. Simmer, covered, until rice is cooked (note that this step can also be done in a rice cooker). Remove from heat.

In another saucepan, scald cream and add chocolate. Stir until it is well mixed and all solids are dissolved. Slowly pour the chocolate mixture into the rice, stirring constantly. Fold in apricots and cranberries. Keep warm until serving time.

Note: Try to make this dish as close to serving time as possible so that it stays creamy and loose.

ROASTED APRICOTS

15 g (0.6 oz) salted butter
6 apricots, pitted
granulated sugar, to taste

Preheat the oven to 150°C (300°F). In an ovenproof pan large enough to hold the apricots, melt butter over low heat. Roll apricots in butter then sprinkle them with sugar. Arrange apricots in the pan and place in the oven. Roast apricots until flesh is soft but fruit still holds its shape. Keep warm until serving time.

VANILLA COOKIES

100 g (3.6 oz) icing sugar
100 g (3.6 oz) all-purpose flour
100 g (3.6 oz) salted butter, softened
1 vanilla bean, split lengthwise
70 g (2.5 oz) egg whites (about 2⅓ large)

Sift together sugar and flour. Using a rubber spatula, mix in butter, vanilla seeds and egg whites. Discard vanilla pod. Refrigerate dough before using.

To bake, preheat oven to 165°C (325°F). Spread a thin even layer of dough onto a silicone mat. Using a decorating comb with square ends (cut the pointed tips out of a regular decorating comb to make the ends square), cut rectangles 10 × 15 cm (4 × 6″). Or make individual cookie strips by spooning the dough into a piping bag and piping the dough into single lines of the same size. Bake until golden brown, about 3 to 5 minutes; then, while still hot, form the rectangles or strips into funky shapes. Cool and store in an airtight container.

Note: Bake the strips a few at a time so you have time to shape them; the cookies will break as you bend them if they are too cool.

GARNISH

125 mL (½ cup) apricot reduction, page 153
125 mL (½ cup) port reduction, page 153
6 scoops apricot sorbet, page 154 (optional)

ASSEMBLY

Drop 2 or more spoonfuls of risotto onto the centre of each plate. Top with an apricot. Drizzle the reductions around the risotto. Decorate with a few cookies. For contrast, serve with a scoop of apricot sorbet.

WINE

A French botrytis-affected Riesling or Canadian VQA Riesling icewine should pair well with the cream and leading apricot flavour of this dessert. These wines possess an intense aroma that ranges from fresh blossoms and apricots to tangerines and candied lime. The flavours are usually very upfront and the wine has a very lively, balanced acidity.

Apple softcake with dark chocolate and cinnamon soup

CINNAMON IS THE KEYNOTE flavour in this dessert. It is an incredible partner for apple and it is the perfect complement for yam (sweet potato or pumpkin would be great alternatives); in this recipe, the yam is roasted to concentrate its natural sweetness. Cinnamon also elevates the sensuous dark chocolate soup to unite the elements in this dish. *Serves 6 to 8*

APPLE SOFTCAKE

250 g (9.1 oz) white chocolate
30 mL (2 Tbsp) apple purée, page 151
60 g (2.1 oz) unsalted butter
75 g (2.7 oz) sweetened condensed milk
75 g (2.7 oz) all-purpose flour
50 g (1.9 oz) ground almonds
2.5 mL (½ tsp) ground cinnamon
4 large eggs

Preheat oven to 190°C (375°F).

Fill a medium saucepan with 5 cm (2″) water and bring to a boil. Turn off the heat but leave the pot on the burner. Combine chocolate, purée and butter in a stainless steel bowl; place the bowl over the pan of hot water for the mixture to melt. Add milk and stir well.

Using a whisk, combine flour, almonds, cinnamon and eggs in a bowl. Fold into the chocolate mixture. Pour batter into 5 cm (2″) round flexible silicone moulds or nonstick tins. Bake for about 15 to 20 minutes. Remove from oven and cool before unmoulding.

ZESTY CHOCOLATE BARK

zest of 1 lemon
zest of 1 orange
zest of 1 lime
200 g (7.2 oz) white chocolate, tempered

Combine zests in a bowl. Spread them evenly on a microwaveable plate and dry on high for 10 seconds. Turn the plate and dry on high for 10 more seconds. Continue turning the plate and heating the zests in 10-second intervals until they are fully dry. Toss them occasionally to make sure they dry evenly. Break up any clumps of dried zests with your hands.

On a sheet of clear acetate or a piece of plastic wrap stretched tight over a board and secured with tape, spread chocolate very thinly with a spatula. Sprinkle evenly with zests. Allow to set (crystallize). Once chocolate is hard, break it into shards. Store in a cool dry place, but do not refrigerate.

DARK CHOCOLATE AND CINNAMON SOUP

125 mL (½ cup) whipping cream
1 cinnamon stick
20 g (0.7 oz) granulated sugar
125 g (4.5 oz) 70% cocoa dark chocolate, finely chopped
200 mL (¾ cup + 1 Tbsp) mineral water

Combine cream and cinnamon in a saucepan; bring to a boil. Remove from heat, cover tightly with plastic wrap to create a natural vacuum, and allow flavours to infuse for at least 1 hour.

Add sugar and bring cream back to a boil, stirring constantly to prevent scorching. Strain cream and discard cinnamon.

Place chocolate in a medium bowl. Pour cream over chocolate and, using a rubber spatula, mix well. Stir in water, then refrigerate until cold.

APPLE SALAD

1 Granny Smith apple, unpeeled
45 mL (3 Tbsp) citrus dressing, page 153

Using a Japanese turning slicer, cut apple into long spaghetti-like strands. Toss apple with dressing. Prepare just before serving so apple stays crisp and white.

GARNISH

6 to 8 scoops yam sorbet, page 155

ASSEMBLY

Cut the top of each softcake at a slight angle and place in the centre of each soup plate. Top with a shard of bark. Place a scoop of sorbet on the bark and top with some apple salad. Serve with a small glass of soup so that guests can pour their own just before eating, or serve the soup in a glass pitcher that can be passed around.

WINE

A sweet fortified Muscat wine, such as Muscat de Beaumes-de-Venise, should complement the chocolate, apple and nut flavours of this dessert. An Elysium, made from the black Muscat grape, with its rather light port quality, is another option.

Crunchy chocolate spring roll with mint and mango salad

EAST MEETS WEST in this playful and exciting display of contrasts. An extra-crisp spring roll wrapper envelops a warm and soft chocolate-hazelnut filling. A sweet and sour citrus dressing coats a cool mint and mango salad. Each mouthful combines a variety of textures and flavours. *Serves 6 (2 rolls per person)*

CHOCOLATE SPRING ROLL

250 mL (1 cup) 2% milk
zest of 1 orange
1.25 mL (¼ tsp) ground cinnamon
3 large egg yolks
60 g (2.1 oz) granulated sugar
25 g (0.9 oz) custard powder
35 g (1.2 oz) icing sugar
35 g (1.2 oz) roasted hazelnuts, finely ground
35 g (1.2 oz) 70% cocoa dark chocolate, melted
six 20 cm (8") square spring roll wrappers
1 large egg, beaten, for egg wash
500 mL (2 cups) oil for deep-frying

Bring milk to a boil in a saucepan. Add zest and cinnamon. Remove from heat, cover tightly with plastic wrap to create a natural vacuum, and allow flavours to infuse for at least 15 minutes.

In a bowl, combine egg yolks, granulated sugar and custard powder; whisk lightly until sugar is dissolved. Strain milk over the egg mixture. Discard the zest.

Cook the mixture over high heat until it forms bubbles and thickens, stirring constantly with a wire whisk to prevent scorching. Remove from heat and pour into a food processor. Add icing sugar, hazelnuts and chocolate. Mix until thoroughly combined. Transfer to a clean, shallow container and cover immediately with plastic wrap pressed right against the mixture. Using the sharp point of a knife, puncture about 6 holes to allow steam to escape. Cool for at least 1 hour, then refrigerate.

Cut each spring roll wrapper in half across and brush one side of each piece completely with egg wash. Pipe or spoon a bead of cool chocolate filling onto the wrapper, about 2.5 cm (1") from the bottom and each side. Fold the bottom and side edges over filling. Brush the newly exposed dough with egg wash. Roll the wrapper into a tight cylinder. Repeat until all wrappers and filling are used up. Freeze for 2 hours, or up to 4 weeks (store in an airtight container for longer periods).

To bake, preheat the oven to 150°C (300°F). Heat a deep fryer to 180°C (350°F). Drop frozen spring rolls into hot oil and fry until golden brown. Remove from oil with a slotted spoon and lay them on a wire rack over a baking sheet. Place in the oven for 5 minutes, or until hot in the centre. Keep warm until serving time.

SWEET AND SOUR SAUCE

100 g (3.6 oz) granulated sugar
15 g (0.6 oz) corn syrup
30 mL (2 Tbsp) water
80 mL (⅓ cup) blood orange juice, page 151

Cook sugar, syrup and water in a saucepan over medium heat until the mixture reaches a caramel colour. Decook with juice. Continue cooking until the mixture is thick and syrupy. Refrigerate.

MINT AND MANGO SALAD

1 large mango, peeled, pitted and cut into 5 mm (¼") dice
60 mL (¼ cup) citrus dressing, page 153
20 g (0.7 oz) fresh peppermint (about 84 large leaves)

Toss mango with ½ of the dressing in a bowl. In a separate bowl, toss peppermint with remaining ½ of the dressing.

ASSEMBLY

Arrange 2 to 3 teaspoonfuls mango in the centre of each plate. Top with a warm spring roll. Spoon a bead of sauce on each side of the roll. Place a small mound of mint atop the roll. Serve immediately.

WINE

A Gewürztraminer, as a French late-harvest or as a Canadian VQA ice-wine, will enhance the spicy notes of the mint and tropical flavours of the mango.

foaming

Foaming is the operation of whipping an egg so that it can trap air. Whipping the egg (whole, white or yolk) breaks or unwinds its protein strands so they can join together while trapping air. When baked, the air cells and the moisture trapped in them turn into steam and expand, allowing the foam to rise. Simultaneously, the proteins around the air cells start to coagulate, providing the foam with the structure it needs to stay up.

In meringues, sponges, soufflés and sabayons—which are basically foams— the eggs are the emulsifying, leavening and / or binding agents, so their temperature and quality are very important. Problems with egg whites are common while foaming; for example, deflation is a common failure in making hot soufflés. Here are some tips to prevent such pitfalls:

WARM TEMPERATURE. Temperature affects the overall time needed to make a foam. Start with eggs at room temperature, or warm them by whisking the eggs over a low-heat water bath before adding them to the recipe. You can also gently heat all sides of the mixing bowl with a blowtorch while the electric mixer is whisking the foam.

FRESH EGGS. Older egg whites yield greater volume, but fresh ones are more stable. Note that leftover egg whites can be frozen to make foams, but they must be thawed slowly overnight in the refrigerator before use.

ADDING SUGAR. Sugar stabilizes foams; however, it should not be added too early. For best results, whip the egg white briefly (30 to 60 seconds) on the highest speed to break up its protein, then continue whipping on medium speed to incorporate as much air as possible. When the foam has nearly reached its full volume, it will no longer rise but cling to the side of the bowl and actually start to slide away from it. At that point, turn up the speed to the highest again and start to incorporate the sugar. When all the sugar has been added, giving the foam a few vigorous turns with a whisk will make the foam more stable during baking.

ADDING ACID. Adding acids, such as cream of tartar, increases stability whereas adding salt decreases it. Salt draws moisture, resulting in drier foams.

Milk chocolate and orange parfait with steamed meringues and orange and black truffle brown butter

⸻

THIS FROZEN PARFAIT combines chocolate and orange in a dessert that is as light as a feathery mousse and perfectly complements the cloud-like softness of steamed meringues. Paired with a chocolate softcake for substance and an outrageous orange and black truffle brown butter sauce for decadence, this dessert is the height of sweet pleasure. *Serves 8 to 10*

MILK CHOCOLATE AND ORANGE PARFAIT

3 large egg yolks
1 large egg
30 mL (2 Tbsp) orange juice, page 151
75 g (2.7 oz) milk chocolate, melted
160 mL (⅔ cup) whipping cream

Combine egg yolks, egg and juice in a stainless steel bowl. Place the bowl over a saucepan of simmering but not boiling water on medium heat, and whisk until the mixture is foamy and reaches 85°C (185°F). Remove from heat and cool to body temperature. Add chocolate and combine well. Set aside.

Whip cream until it forms soft peaks. Using a rubber spatula, gently fold cream into the chocolate mixture. Pour into 5 cm (2″) round or oval flexible silicone moulds or metal rings lined with strips of silicone paper. Freeze.

STEAMED MERINGUES

100 g (3.6 oz) egg whites (about 3 large)
100 g (3.6 oz) granulated sugar

Preheat the oven to 180°C (350°F).

Using an electric mixer fitted with a whisk, beat egg whites. As soon as foam starts to slide from the sides of the bowl and no longer gains volume, add sugar slowly. Continue beating until egg whites form stiff peaks.

Spoon the meringue into a piping bag fitted with a plain round tube. Pipe into 5 cm (2″) round flexible silicone moulds or nonstick tins. Cover with a sheet of aluminum foil that has been punched with holes, making sure that the foil does not touch the meringue. Place in a bain-marie and bake for about 20 minutes. Cool and unmould onto a silicone mat or paper. Serve at room temperature.

Note: This meringue does not last very long and should be made no more than a few hours before serving.

CHOCOLATE SOFTCAKES

125 g (4.5 oz) 70% cocoa dark chocolate
50 g (1.9 oz) salted butter
2 large egg yolks
125 g (4.5 oz) egg whites (about 4 large)
25 g (0.9 oz) granulated sugar

Fill a medium saucepan with 5 cm (2″) water and bring to a boil. Turn off the heat but leave the pot on the burner. Combine chocolate and butter in a stainless steel bowl; place the bowl over the pan of hot water for the mixture to melt. Cool to body temperature then whisk in egg yolks. Set aside.

Using an electric mixer fitted with a whisk, beat egg whites. As soon as foam starts to slide from the sides of the bowl and no longer gains volume, add sugar slowly.

Continue beating until egg whites form stiff peaks.

Using a rubber spatula, gently fold egg whites into the chocolate mixture. Pour batter into 5 cm (2″) round flexible silicone moulds or nonstick tins and freeze.

To bake, preheat the oven to 200°C (400°F). Remove moulds from freezer and bake, still frozen, for about 8 to 10 minutes. Softcakes are done when they start to rise. Remove from oven and cool before unmoulding.

ORANGE AND BLACK TRUFFLE BROWN BUTTER

150 g (5.3 oz) salted butter
15 mL (1 Tbsp) black truffle oil
60 mL (¼ cup) frozen orange juice concentrate

Make a brown butter by cooking butter in a heavy saucepan over low heat. When butter starts to foam, milk solids at the bottom of the pan start to turn brown (but are not burned), and mixture has a pleasant nutty odour, remove it from heat. Pour into a tall narrow container. Just before serving, emulsify butter with oil and juice using a high-speed or immersion blender. Serve warm.

COCOA STICKS

14 g (0.5 oz) corn syrup
60 mL (¼ cup) simple syrup, page 152
40 g (1.4 oz) unsweetened cocoa powder, sifted

Preheat the oven to 165°C (325°F).

Bring syrups to a boil in a heavy saucepan. Pour over cocoa in a small bowl and mix well. Spoon the mixture into a disposable plastic piping bag. Cut a small hole at the tip of the bag. Pipe into funky curved lines on a silicone mat. Bake for about 5 minutes. While still soft, bend sticks into interesting shapes. Or, cool sticks on a silicone mat and use broken pieces as garnish. Store in an airtight container.

Note: Place soft or limp sticks in a 165°C (325°F) oven for few minutes to crisp them.

GARNISH

30 g (1.1 oz) caramelized walnut pieces, page 156

ASSEMBLY

Place a parfait a little off centre on each plate. Cut a meringue in half lengthwise and place one piece on top of the parfait. Cut a softcake in half lengthwise. Stand the pieces behind the parfait, leaning against it. Top the meringue with a few cocoa sticks and garnish with walnuts. Spoon brown butter behind the soft-cake. Serve immediately.

WINE

A sweet fortified wine, such as Muscat de Beaumes-de-Venise, California black Muscat or orange Muscat, should pair well with the chocolate, orange and nut flavours of this dessert.

White chocolate and yogurt mousse mille-feuille

SINFULLY CREAMY white chocolate mousse is paired with the sweet tartness of salmonberries and the slight acidity of yogurt to create a dessert that is pure decadence. Sandwiched between layers of crunchy feuille de brick and topped with a refreshing orange sorbet, this melt-in-the-mouth mousse mille-feuille is deceptively simple to make yet tastes extravagant. *Serves 6 to 8*

WHITE CHOCOLATE AND YOGURT MOUSSE

175 g (6.3 oz) white chocolate

150 g (5.3 oz) plain (natural) yogurt, at room temperature

4 g (2) gelatin leaves, bloomed

200 mL (¾ cup + 1 Tbsp) whipping cream (in soft peaks)

Melt white chocolate over a double boiler or in a microwave oven. Set aside.

Heat ⅓ of the yogurt in a microwave oven on high in 20-second intervals; warm until yogurt reaches 60°C (125°F). Add gelatin and stir until completely dissolved. Add to chocolate with remaining yogurt and mix until all ingredients are thoroughly combined. Cool the mixture to about 30°C (86°F) and, with a rubber spatula, fold in cream. Allow to set in fridge, covered with a sheet of plastic wrap.

FEUILLE DE BRICK MILLE-FEUILLES

nine 25 cm (10″) round sheets of feuille de brick (available in North African specialty stores, or substitute phyllo but it will produce a different texture and appearance)

125 g (4.5 oz) salted butter, melted

granulated sugar, to taste

Preheat the oven to 180°C (350°F). Lay 1 sheet of feuille de brick on a clean and dry surface and brush with melted butter. Sprinkle with sugar. Lay another sheet on top, brush with butter and sprinkle with sugar. Repeat with a third sheet. Using special artist scissors to create a unique trim, cut shapes from the layered sheets. Do the same for the other sheets remaining. Bake on a silicone mat for 5 to 10 minutes, or until golden brown.

WHITE CHOCOLATE DÉCOR

100 g (3.6 oz) white chocolate, finely chopped

In a food processor, mix chocolate until it comes together and forms a ball.

Roll chocolate flat to a thickness of about 2 mm (⅛″) on a silicone mat. Cut out 6 to 8 pleasing 5 cm (2″) shapes, leaving the edges ragged to give them a more rustic look. While still soft, bend décors into three-dimensional shapes with lots of curves.

GARNISH

125 mL (½ cup) raspberry reduction, page 154

6 to 8 scoops orange sorbet, page 155

80 mL (⅓ cup) salmonberry gelée, page 153, frozen and cut into 5 mm (¼″) cubes

50 mL (3 Tbsp + 1 tsp) orange oil, page 151

ASSEMBLY

Spoon a bead of reduction onto the centre of each plate. Place a feuille de brick mille-feuille in the middle of that bead and, using an ice cream scoop, top with a dome of mousse. Layer another feuille de brick mille-feuille on the mousse, and top the mille-feuille with a scoop of sorbet. Arrange a few gelée cubes on the sorbet and garnish with the décor. Drizzle a few drops of orange oil around the plate. Serve immediately.

WINE

An orange Muscat from France or California or a sparkling Moscato d'Asti from Italy should complement the creamy texture of the mousse and the orange flavour of the sorbet. Remember, each of these wines will do something different to the dessert; this would be a great dish with which to experiment.

Warm chocolate blinis with yellow pepper and mango compote

YELLOW PEPPERS for dessert? Yes, indeed. Sweet peppers are fruit and their sweetness makes them more appropriate for desserts than one would think. This utterly sublime dish unites incredibly soft and decadent chocolate blinis, lusciously sexy lemon vodka cream and zesty yellow pepper and mango compote. Each component can be made several days ahead so you can assemble and serve this dessert in just minutes. *Serves 6 to 8*

WARM CHOCOLATE BLINIS

85 g (3.1 oz) 70% cocoa dark chocolate, melted
40 g (1.4 oz) milk chocolate, melted
25 g (0.9 oz) unsalted butter, melted
2.5 mL (½ tsp) ground cinnamon
2.5 mL (½ tsp) ground cardamom
120 g (4.3 oz) egg whites (about 4 large)
50 g (1.9 oz) granulated sugar
60 g (2.1 oz) milk chocolate, finely chopped

Preheat the oven to 180°C (350°F). Mix melted chocolates, butter, cinnamon and cardamom. Set aside.

Using an electric mixer fitted with a whisk, beat egg whites. As soon as foam starts to slide from the sides of the bowl and no longer gains volume, add sugar slowly. Continue beating until egg whites form stiff peaks.

Using a rubber spatula, gently fold ⅓ of the egg whites into the melted chocolate mixture. Gently fold in the remaining egg whites. Just before egg whites are completely combined, fold in chopped chocolate.

Spoon the mixture into a piping bag fitted with a plain round tube. Pipe into 5 cm (2″) round mounds on a silicone mat or paper. Bake for about 6 minutes. Set aside until serving time or freeze, well covered, for several weeks.

YELLOW PEPPER AND MANGO COMPOTE

1 small sweet yellow pepper
125 mL (½ cup) simple syrup, page 152
5 mL (1 tsp) powdered pectin
1 mango, peeled and pitted

With a blowtorch or over an open flame, char the skin on the pepper. Peel skin with the back of a paring knife. Discard skin, membranes and seeds. Chop the flesh into 5 mm (¼″) dice.

Bring syrup to a boil. Briefly poach peppers, making sure that flesh remains whole and al dente. Drain and reserve syrup. Set peppers aside.

Mix pectin with 30 mL (2 Tbsp) reserved syrup. Dissolve in a microwave oven on high. Purée the mango in a food processor. With the motor running, pour in the pectin mixture and continue mixing until it thickens. Combine mango purée with peppers and refrigerate.

LEMON BALM EMULSION

200 mL (¾ cup + 1 Tbsp) whole milk
50 g (1.9 oz) fresh lemon balm
zest of 1 lemon
3 large egg yolks
2 large eggs

75 g (2.7 oz) granulated sugar
2.5 g (1¼) gelatin leaves, bloomed
45 mL (3 Tbsp) lemon vodka
75 g (2.7 oz) salted butter, at room temperature

Combine milk, lemon balm and zest in a saucepan; bring to a boil. Remove from heat, cover tightly with plastic wrap to create a natural vacuum, and allow flavours to infuse for at least 30 minutes.

In a bowl, combine egg yolks, eggs and sugar; whisk lightly until sugar is dissolved.

Strain milk, making sure that you have 125 mL (½ cup), and discard balm and zest. Pour into the egg mixture a little at a time, whisking constantly. Cook the mixture until it starts to boil, stirring constantly to prevent scorching. Remove from heat and add gelatin, stirring well to combine. Cool the mixture to body temperature over an ice-water bath. Stir in vodka.

Place butter in a food processor. With the motor running, slowly pour in milk mixture a little at a time so that it emulsifies and thickens. Refrigerate.

Note: For best re-warming results, place emulsion on a microwaveable dish and warm in 15-second intervals before serving. Stir between intervals. Repeat until the mixture is warmed.

WHITE CHOCOLATE DÉCOR

125 g (½ cup) white chocolate,
   tempered

Freeze a marble slab or a ceramic
tile overnight.

Fill a disposable plastic piping
bag with some tempered chocolate.
Cut a small hole at the tip of the
bag. On the frozen marble slab or
tile, pipe chocolate back and forth to
obtain 6 to 10 thin strands. Pick up
the strands together and twist them
into a nest shape or a loop. Repeat

to make 6 to 8 décors. Work quickly
or the strands will set and become
too hard to bend. Place décors on a
baking sheet to harden (crystallize)
fully, then store in a cool, dry place
until serving time.

GARNISH

6 to 8 quenelles mango sorbet,
   page 154

ASSEMBLY

Spoon a small pool of emulsion
onto the centre of each plate. Place
a blini in the middle of the emulsion

and top with a spoonful of compote.
Place a quenelle of sorbet atop the
compote, layer on another blini,
and finish with a décor. Serve
immediately.

WINE

A Canadian VQA Riesling icewine
or a late-harvest of the same varietal
should pair well with the tropical
and zesty notes of this dessert. A
well-made Asti Spumante is another
option.

Dark chocolate "six façons"

———— ⊗⊗⊗ ————

CHOCOLATE SIX WAYS is pure opulence! This modern, playfully presented dessert features 70% cocoa dark chocolate in a careful sequence that will introduce you to tastes and textures you never thought possible. Begin with a feathery light foam, then indulge in a soft and oven-hot chocoufflé. Contrast this with a crunchy frozen sorbet, followed by a warm and airy softcake. Then bite into a hot crispy croquette before finishing with a cold creamy malted milk.

Whether you make all six desserts to treat yourself, make slightly larger portions or individual samplers and host a dessert party, or make just one dessert and try it on its own, chocolate six façons will surprise and delight you. *Serves 12*

ONE: CHOCOLATE FOAM

250 mL (1 cup) whipping cream
120 g (4.3 oz) 70% cocoa dark
  chocolate, chopped
150 g (5.3 oz) fresh banana purée,
  page 151
40 g (1.4 oz) egg whites (about
  1½ large)

Boil cream in a saucepan. Pour it over chocolate, stirring with a rubber spatula until all solids dissolve. Add purée and egg whites. Strain, and discard solids. Pour the liquid into a siphon cream dispenser and add nitrous oxide. Refrigerate.

GARNISH

12 sesame and walnut croustillants, page 156, cut into 5 cm (2″) ovals or rounds
30 g (1.1 oz) caramelized walnut pieces, page 156

SERVICE

Just before serving time, dispense some foam into a cup. Form a quenelle of foam with a soup spoon, and place it on a croustillant. Top with a few walnuts. Serve immediately.

TWO: CHOCOUFFLÉ

80 mL (⅓ cup) 2% milk
15 g (0.6 oz) unsweetened
  cocoa powder
6 g (0.3 oz) all-purpose flour
60 g (2.1 oz) egg yolks (about 3 large)
65 g (2.4 oz) granulated sugar
1 g (½) gelatin leaf, bloomed
15 g (0.6 oz) 70% cocoa dark chocolate, finely chopped
45 g (1.6 oz) egg whites (about
  1½ large)

Line a 15 cm (6″) square pan with plastic wrap, or, for best results, use 5 cm (2″) oval or 3.75 cm (1½″) round flexible silicone moulds.

Warm milk, cocoa and flour in a saucepan over medium heat.

In a bowl, whisk egg yolks with ½ of the sugar. Stir into the milk mixture, and cook, stirring constantly, until the mixture thickens to the consistency of a stirred custard. Remove from heat. Add gelatin and chocolate.

Using an electric mixer fitted with a whisk, beat egg whites until they form soft peaks. As soon as foam starts to slide from the sides of the bowl and no longer gains volume, gradually add the other ½ of the sugar.

Using a rubber spatula, fold ⅓ of the egg whites into chocolate to loosen the mixture. Fold in the remaining egg whites until all ingredients are well combined.

Pour the batter into the pan or moulds to a depth of 1.25 cm (½″). Smooth the tops as flat as possible. Freeze.

To bake, preheat the oven to 180°C (350°F). Remove frozen chocoufflés from moulds, or use a cookie cutter to make squares or rounds. Place individual frozen desserts (refreeze them if they have gone soft) on a silicone mat and bake for 10 to 15 minutes. Serve immediately.

GARNISH

12 Bing cherries, quartered
125 mL (½ cup) citrus reduction, page 153
1 recipe chocolate gelée, page 153
12 small pieces of gold leaf (optional)

SERVICE

Place four cherry quarters on the base of a dish. Drizzle with reduction. Top with a hot chocoufflé, some chocolate gelée and, if desired, a gold leaf.

continued overleaf

THREE: CHOCOLATE SORBET WITH MERINGUE

CHOCOLATE MERINGUE

50 g (1.9 oz) egg whites (about
    1½ large)
50 g (1.9 oz) granulated sugar
50 g (1.9 oz) icing sugar
10 g (0.4 oz) unsweetened
    cocoa powder

Preheat the oven to 100°C (200°F).
Using an electric mixer fitted with
a whisk, beat egg whites until they
form stiff peaks. As soon as foam
starts to slide from the sides of the
bowl and no longer gains volume,
add granulated sugar slowly.

Sift together icing sugar and
cocoa. Using a rubber spatula, fold
the cocoa mixture into beaten egg
whites. Spoon the meringue into a
piping bag fitted with a plain round
tube. Pipe 12 individual 5 cm (2″)
ovals onto a silicone mat. Bake for

about 1 hour. Cool and store in an
airtight container for up to 2 weeks.

GARNISH

12 scoops or quenelles chocolate
sorbet, page 154

SERVICE

Place a meringue in the centre of
each plate. Top each with a scoop of
sorbet. Serve immediately.

FOUR: SOFTCAKE

6 chocolate softcakes, page 108, cut
    into 5 cm (2″) oval flexible silicone
    moulds
80 mL (⅓ cup) tangerine gelée, page
    153, with 10 g (0.4 oz) of finely
    chopped and sifted nibs of 70%
    cocoa dark chocolate added just
    before setting
1 tangerine, peeled, seeded and
    segmented

SERVICE

Slice a softcake in half to form 2
semicircles. Place one half in the
centre of a dish. Spoon some gelée
in front of the cake. Garnish the
top of the cake with small pieces of
tangerine.

Note: Mandarin or navel oranges
can be used instead of tangerines.

FIVE: CHOCOLATE CROQUETTE

CHOCOLATE CROQUETTE

1–2 phyllo sheets
45–90 g (1.6–3.2 oz) salted butter,
    melted
12 maple whisky truffles, page 143,
    whisky omitted, and truffle mix-
    ture frozen in a 10 × 2.5 × 1.25 cm
    (4 × 1 × ½″) pan then, when
    frozen, cut into 1.25 × 2.5 × 1.25
    cm (½ × 1 × ½″) pieces
30–60 g egg whites (about 1–2 large)
125 g (4.5 oz) panko bread crumbs
500 mL (2 cups) oil for deep-frying

Lay 1 sheet of phyllo on a clean
and dry surface and brush with melted butter. Cut phyllo into 10 cm (4″)
squares and place a piece of frozen
ganache in the middle of each. Fold
the two sides of phyllo over the
ganache. Fold the bottom edge of
the phyllo over the ganache and roll
into a tight parcel. Moisten the top
edge of the phyllo and press lightly
to seal. Brush the parcels with egg
whites, then roll them in the bread
crumbs. Freeze on baking sheets.

Preheat the oven to 180°C (350°F). Heat a deep fryer to 180°C (350°F). Drop parcels in hot oil and fry until golden brown. Remove from oil with a slotted spoon and lay them on a wire rack over a baking sheet. Place in the oven for a few minutes to finish cooking until centre is hot. Keep warm until serving time.

GARNISH

24 lychees, quartered

45 mL (3 Tbsp) citrus dressing, page 153

SERVICE

Toss lychees in dressing and arrange at the bottom of a dish. Top with a croquette and serve immediately.

SIX: MALT DRINK

100 mL (⅓ cup + 1 Tbsp) whipping cream

100 mL (⅓ cup + 1 Tbsp) 2% milk

100 g (3.6 oz) 70% cocoa dark chocolate, finely chopped

30 g (1.1 oz) malt powder

10 mL (2 tsp) instant coffee grounds

50 g (1.9 oz) vanilla ice cream, page 20

Bring cream and milk to a boil in a saucepan.

In a bowl, combine chocolate, malt powder and coffee. Pour the cream mixture on top, mix to combine, and allow to cool.

Just before serving, emulsify the chocolate mixture with ice cream using a high-speed or immersion blender. Serve immediately in a glass container.

"SIX FAÇONS" ASSEMBLY

Use a sectioned plate, and arrange the six desserts in the sequence listed above. Use an individual compartment for each dessert.

WINE

Since this dish has so many different components, suggesting a single wine is rather difficult. If we had to select only one, we'd recommend a fortified Muscat-based wine, perhaps a Liqueur Muscat or Liqueur Tokay from Australia. The notes range from dried fruit, nuts, coffee and toffee through to cardamom and ginger. Although not as direct, consider also an Elysium, made from the black Muscat grape; it has a rather light port quality to it.

grains and seeds

The fields

—∞∞∞—

Desserts and sweets are often considered rewards, foods that we indulge in and then feel guilty about eating because they are full of fat and sugar. However, a dazzling dessert can be healthy, and grains and seeds—the seed-like fruit or the single seeds of a plant—are often the key. Used as a food source for thousands of years, grains and seeds are highly nutritious and much lower in fat than nuts, though they can be similar in taste. Toasting grains and seeds before cooking brings out a strong nutty flavour, and they contribute considerably less fat to a finished dish than nuts do. All three foods—grains, seeds and nuts—are full of monounsaturated and polyunsaturated fatty acids, a healthier alternative to the saturated fatty acids typically found in heavier, mostly dairy-based desserts.

In addition to satisfying our nutritional needs and our concern for healthier sweets, grains and seeds create modern desserts that are innovative, complexly flavoured and full of texture. These foods range in flavour from earthy wheat or corn-like tastes to nutty notes. But their richness and texture are their most valuable qualities. Delicately soft, chewy, crispy, dense, firm, crumbly—such a broad range of textures and "bulk" results in a whole variety of brilliant grain-based desserts.

Be creative. You can make exotic desserts using such common grains as rice, but we also provide some examples using more unusual ingredients such as red tapioca pearls, polenta, red lentils and wheat berries. Try quinoa, a tiny bead-shaped grain from South America, as a wonderful alternative to rice in a sweet risotto. Or consider amaranth—once considered a simple weed—in delicate and tasty wafers or in place of rice in a sweet pudding or risotto. Other exotic varieties, such as wild rice, kamut and spelt, could easily be used instead of, or in conjunction with, wheat berry or rice.

119

Maple wine and cherimoya frappé with orange blossom fingers

———— ⬤⬤⬤ ————

ON A VISIT to Hong Kong a few years ago, we were introduced to an incredibly refreshing concoction called bubble tea, a cool, sweet fruit drink made from fresh fruit, crushed ice and tapioca pearls. This is our version. The large red tapioca pearls add substance to the ice cold cherimoya frappé, which is sweetened with Canadian maple wine. Warm and crispy orange blossom fingers complete the experience. *Serves 6*

CANDIED TAPIOCA PEARLS
250 mL (1 cup) water
50 g (1.9 oz) red tapioca pearls
125 mL (½ cup) simple syrup,
    page 152

Bring water to a boil; pour in the tapioca pearls and continue boiling for 30 minutes. Remove from heat, cover saucepan tightly with plastic wrap to create a natural vacuum, and allow to sit at room temperature for 30 minutes.

Drain tapioca. Transfer to a container with a tight-fitting lid. Add syrup and refrigerate, covered, for 1 hour. Pearls will keep in the fridge for several days.

MAPLE WINE AND CHERIMOYA FRAPPÉ
1 cherimoya (custard apple), seeded,
    flesh scooped out with a spoon
80 mL (⅓ cup) Canadian maple wine
125 mL (½ cup) whole milk
125 g (4.5 oz) ice cubes

Just before serving, place cherimoya, wine, milk and ice in a heavy-duty high-speed blender (a Vita-Mix®–type machine works best). Blend on highest speed until all ingredients are homogeneous and ice is completely chopped. Serve immediately.

ORANGE BLOSSOM FINGERS
5 g (0.25 oz) dry yeast
60 mL (¼ cup) warm whole milk
1 large egg
25 g (0.9 oz) granulated sugar
50 g (1.9 oz) salted butter, softened
5 mL (1 tsp) orange blossom water
125 g (4.5 oz) all-purpose flour, sifted
1 L (4 cups) oil for deep-frying
icing sugar for dusting

Dissolve yeast in warm milk, stirring constantly until yeast is completely dissolved.

In a bowl, combine egg, sugar, butter and orange blossom water, mixing with a rubber spatula until thoroughly incorporated. Pour in the yeast mixture and mix well. Fold in the flour.

Place the dough on a floured surface and knead gently for about 1 minute, or until the dough is smooth and shiny. Return the dough to the bowl, cover tightly with plastic wrap, and refrigerate for a few hours, or until the dough has at least doubled in size. Place a cutting board in the fridge to chill.

On a cold, floured surface, roll the dough as thin as possible, about 2 mm (⅛″). Transfer the sheet of dough to a cutting board and place in the freezer until dough is almost completely frozen, about 1 to 4 hours.

To cook, preheat a deep fryer to 180°C (350°F). Remove the dough from the freezer and cut into 8.75 cm (3 ½″) wide strips. Divide into 1.25 × 8.75 cm (½ × 3½″) rectangles. Cut rectangles on the diagonal to make triangles. Drop in hot oil and fry until golden brown. Remove from oil with a slotted spoon and drain on a paper towel for a few seconds. Keep warm. Dust with sugar just before serving.

CHOCOLATE SPAGHETTI
100 g (3.6 oz) 70% cocoa dark
    chocolate, tempered

Place a sheet of silicone or waxed paper on a clean, level surface. Plunge a dinner knife about halfway into chocolate. Drag knife across the paper to form thin strands. Allow to set (crystallize) in a cool, dry place but do not refrigerate. Peel paper from chocolate. Serve, or store in an airtight container in a cool, dry place. Spaghetti will keep for up to 1 month.

ASSEMBLY
Set a martini-type glass in the centre of each soup plate. Fill the glass to ⅓ full with tapioca pearls. Pour frappé on top and garnish with some spaghetti. Arrange orange blossom fingers around the foot of the glass. Serve immediately.

WINE
The secret to a perfect wine pairing is to use the wine you want to pair as an ingredient in the recipe. As this dessert already contains a large amount of unprocessed wine, it does not really need pairing. However, should you want to, a Canadian maple wine would be the best option.

caramelization

Caramelization, or making caramel, is the operation of heating a sugar mixture until it liquefies and changes from a thin, clear syrup to progressively thicker and darker shades of brown. The most common way to do this is to heat sugar and water on a stovetop; the sugar is caramelized when the mixture starts to smoke and its surface is thick and foamy. A safer, easier way to do this is using a microwave oven. Place all ingredients in a glass container and cook on high heat, making sure you remove the caramel *before* it reaches the desired colour, since it will continue to cook once it has been removed from the oven. Sugar (white or brown) can also be caramelized by sprinkling it on food and then heating the dish under a radiant heat source such as a broiler. (A blowtorch, with its intense and focused flame, is easier to use when caramelizing surfaces, for example the tops of crèmes brûlées.)

Crystallization is the leading problem in caramel-making. Granulated sugar (also called sucrose) is a double sugar, or disaccharide, made from fructose and glucose, two simple sugars (monosaccharides) that are joined together. During the caramelizing process, the sucrose starts to melt, and as it does it breaks down into new sugars and other compounds. When these new sugars do not dissolve, crystallization occurs.

Here are some tips for preventing crystallization:

ADDING SUGAR OR ACID. Adding a similar yet distinct sugar, such as corn syrup (which is mostly glucose), and/or a few drops of an acid—such as lemon juice, vinegar or cream of tartar—to the mixture will inhibit crystallization.

WASHING THE POT. Washing the sides of the pot with a pastry brush dipped in cold water will dissolve any potential crystals. Or start by cooking the sugar mixture covered with a lid for a couple of minutes so that the water will steam inside the chamber and condense, washing down the sides as it falls back into the sugar.

OILING THE POT. Rubbing the sides of the pot with oil will prevent crystals from clinging. It will also make the caramel easier to pour once it is cooked.

Lemon crépaze with red lentil confit and crispy apple pasta

━━━◯❀❀◯━━━

MEMORIES ARE A GREAT SOURCE of inspiration. Crépaze is a dessert that Dominique's mother used to make when he was a child in Belgium. The success of this dessert lies in the crêpes, which must be lacy thin. Our modern version is filled with an intensely perfumed and delectably creamy lemon-apple emulsion, and accompanied by an incredible red lentil confit and fresh lemon balm emulsion. This dish is indeed a memorable treat! *Serves 8*

LEMON CRÉPAZE

1 large egg
2 large egg yolks
180 mL (¾ cup) 2% milk
20 g (0.7 oz) granulated sugar
85 g (3.1 oz) all-purpose flour, sifted
40 g (1.4 oz) salted butter, melted
455 g (16.4 oz) lemon-apple
    emulsion, page 152

Combine egg, egg yolks and milk in a bowl; beat until well mixed. In a separate bowl, combine sugar and flour. Make a well in the centre and fill it with the egg mixture; mix quickly with a whisk until thoroughly combined.

Make a brown butter by cooking butter in a heavy saucepan over low heat. When butter starts to foam, milk solids at the bottom of the pan start to turn brown (but are not burned), and the mixture smells nutty, remove from heat. Pour it over the batter and mix well. Allow to stand for about 30 minutes.

For best results, lightly spray a nonstick crêpe pan with oil. Heat the pan over medium heat, remove it from the stove and pour some batter into the centre of the pan. Quickly swirl the pan to make sure the batter is evenly and thinly distributed. Return the pan to the stove and cook crepe until it is lightly browned.

Flip crêpe and cook the other side slightly. Slide cooked crêpe onto a plate and repeat this process until all the batter is cooked.

To build the crépaze, place a crêpe in a cake ring that is the same diameter as the crêpe. Spread a thin layer of emulsion evenly on crêpe. Repeat the process, alternating layers until all the cream and crêpes are used. Press firmly on top crêpe to make sure cream permeates all holes in crêpes and that the crépaze is evenly flat. Freeze the crépaze until firm to make cutting easier. Cut into 2.5 × 5 cm (1 × 2″) rectangles, thaw, and refrigerate until serving time.

Note: For less waste, use a Japanese-style square or rectangle frying pan, or cut as wedges.

RED LENTIL CONFIT

10 g (0.4 oz) granulated sugar
200 mL (¾ cup + 1 Tbsp) water
zest of ¼ lemon
¼ vanilla bean, split lengthwise
2.5 mL (½ tsp) fresh ginger, finely
    grated
50 g (1.9 oz) red lentils
1 medium Granny Smith apple,
    peeled, cored and cubed

Combine sugar, water, zest, vanilla seeds and ginger in a saucepan; bring to a boil. Remove from heat, cover with plastic wrap to form a natural vacuum, and allow flavours to infuse for 15 minutes.

In another pot, cook lentils in at least 250 mL (1 cup) water until soft, about 15 to 20 minutes after water has come to a boil. Drain and cool. Set aside.

Add apples to syrup and bring the mixture to a boil. Cook until apples are soft and most of the liquid has evaporated. Stir lentils into the apple mixture and cook for a few minutes to allow flavours to blend. Cool and refrigerate confit overnight.

CRISPY APPLE PASTA

1 medium Granny Smith apple
10 g (0.4 oz) granulated sugar
15 mL (1 Tbsp) lemon juice
10 g (0.4 oz) salted butter, melted
30 g (1.1 oz) granulated sugar

Preheat the oven to 130°C (275°F).

Wash the apple. Using a Japanese turning slicer, cut apple into long spaghetti-like strands. Place strands in a bowl and toss with 10 g (0.4 oz) sugar, juice and butter.

Set a 5 cm (2″) metal ring mould or a circle drawn on a piece of paper under a silicone mat. Untangle tossed apple strands and place a small mound in the mould or on the mat to form a solid, filled-in disk. Repeat with remaining apple strands to make 8 disks. Sprinkle disks with 30 g (1.1 oz) sugar and bake for about 40 minutes, or until apple strands

are dry and crisp. Cool on a wire rack and store in an airtight container at room temperature.

Note: If the strands become soft, reheat them briefly in a 130°C (275°F) oven.

GARNISH

8 lemon and mint oil sucrées, page 137, cut to 2.5 × 5 cm (1 × 2″)
8 sprigs fresh lemon balm (or mint)
60 mL (¼ cup) lemon balm emulsion, page 152

ASSEMBLY

Place a sucrée in the centre of each plate and top with crépaze. Make a quenelle of confit and place on top of the crépaze (or spoon some confit directly on top). Garnish with a sprig of lemon balm and apple pasta. Spoon emulsion on either side of crépaze. Serve immediately.

WINE

A Riesling Beerenauslese, Trockenbeerenauslese, Canadian VQA Riesling icewine or French botrytisaffected Chenin Blanc such as Bonnezeaux or Quarts de Chaume should pair well with the apple flavours of this dessert.

Riso galette with ginger-braised Hon pears

———— ⟨⟨⟨ ————

WHEN PEARS are in season, try this elegant dessert which combines three types of pear with spicy fresh ginger, fragrant desert-flower honey and aromatic vanilla. Sample the delights of the sweet cactus (prickly) pear, perfumed Chinese Hon (fragrance) pear and smooth Comice pear served with a creamy rice galette and crunchy lace. *Serves 6*

RISO GALETTE
10 g (0.4 oz) salted butter
50 g (1.9 oz) short-grain rice
2 g (0.1 oz) fresh ginger, finely grated
250 mL (1 cup) whole milk
150 mL (½ cup + 2 Tbsp) Comice
 pear purée, page 151
30 g (1.1 oz) granulated sugar
20 g (0.7 oz) salted butter

Heat 10 g (0.4 oz) butter in a heavy saucepan over medium heat. Add rice and ginger and sauté 2 to 3 minutes until grains are well coated. Slowly add milk and purée a little at a time. Continue adding liquid a little at a time until it has all been absorbed, about 20 minutes. The risotto should be al dente. Stir in sugar. Spoon mixture into individual 7.5 cm (3″) ring moulds. Refrigerate.

Just before serving, heat 20 g (0.7 oz) butter in a nonstick pan. Pan-fry galettes until golden brown on both sides and warm throughout. Remove from heat and drain on a paper towel. Cut each galette in ½ to create two semicircles. Using a 4 cm (1½″) cookie cutter, cut a semi-circle out of the centre of each ½. Set aside all shapes.

GINGER-BRAISED HON PEARS AND REDUCTION
500 mL (2 cups) water
250 g (9.1 oz) granulated sugar
juice of 1 lemon
1 vanilla bean, split lengthwise
45 g (1.6 oz) desert-flower honey
10 g (0.4 oz) fresh ginger, grated
6 Chinese Hon pears, peeled

Combine water, sugar, juice, vanilla seeds and pod, honey and ginger in a large saucepan; bring to a boil. Reduce heat to low, add pears, cover, and braise for about 20 minutes. Remove from heat, cover saucepan tightly with plastic wrap to create a natural vacuum (to keep flavours in while preventing oxidation), and refrigerate overnight.

Just before serving, remove vanilla pod. Set it aside for garnish. Reheat pears in their cooking juice. Using a slotted spoon, remove pears. Set aside and keep warm.

If you are making the lace for this dish, measure 50 mL (3 Tbsp + 2 tsp) cooking juice and set aside. Reduce remaining cooking juice until the mixture is thick and syrupy. Keep warm until serving time.

PEAR LACE
50 mL (3 Tbsp + 1 tsp) reserved Hon
 pear cooking juice (above)
zest of 1 orange
65 g (2.4 oz) granulated sugar
25 g (0.9 oz) all-purpose flour
25 g (0.9 oz) salted butter, melted

Preheat the oven to 180°C (350°F).
In a large bowl, combine cooking juice, zest, sugar and flour. Mix well. Fold in butter.

Using the back of a spoon, spread about 2.5 mL (½ tsp) of dough onto a silicone mat, making a 5 cm (2″) circle. Repeat to make 9 circles. Bake 4 to 6 minutes, or until golden brown and lacy looking. Cool on mat. Store in an airtight container.

Note: The dough can be refrigerated for several days or frozen for several months. For best results, thaw frozen dough in the refrigerator overnight before using.

GARNISH
6 quenelles or scoops cactus pear
 sorbet, page 154
1 vanilla pod (above), cut into thin
 7.5 cm (3″) sticks

ASSEMBLY
Place a galette semicircle on the left side of each plate. Place a warm pear in the cavity. Spike 3 small shards of lace in one end of pear. Spoon reduction onto opposite end. Place a quenelle or scoop of sorbet on a galette cutout and place it on the right side of the plate. Top sorbet with a stick of vanilla. Serve immediately.

WINE
A French Sauternes (or Sauternes-style), European eiswein or Canadian VQA Gewürztraminer icewine should pair well with the honey, pear and spicy ginger flavours of this dessert.

Grilled pear steak with polenta frites and orange-tarragon sauce

— ◇◇◇ —

A PLAYFUL REINTERPRETATION of a timeless culinary classic, this sweet steak and frites is as comforting as its savoury relative. Soft polenta frites coated with crispy toasted almonds exquisitely contrast the soft, juicy pear steak. The slightly salty Cambozola fondant superbly matches the tangy fresh oranges. *Serves 6 to 8*

GRILLED PEAR STEAK
3 or 4 medium unpeeled Bosc pears
juice of 1 large lemon
olive oil for spraying

Preheat barbecue to high. Preheat the oven to 150° C (300° F).

Cut 2 thick slices of pear from each side, avoiding pear core. Discard core. Rub slices with juice and, using a spray pump, spray lightly with oil. Place pears cut-side down on a barbecue, pressing pears against grill to mark them. Transfer to a baking sheet and cook cut-side up in the oven until pear is soft and a knife inserted in the flesh comes out easily. Keep warm until serving time.

POLENTA FRITES
500 mL (2 cups) fruit stock, page 151
pinch of salt
2 star anise
100 g (3.6 oz) yellow cornmeal
45 g (1.6 oz) unsalted butter
60 mL (¼ cup) 2% milk
100 g (3.6 oz) almonds, ground
125 mL (½ cup) olive or vegetable oil

Line a 15 × 20 cm (6 × 8″) shallow baking pan with plastic wrap.

Combine stock, salt and star anise in a saucepan; bring to a boil. Remove from heat, cover tightly with plastic wrap to create a natural vacuum, and allow flavours to infuse for 10 minutes. Strain and discard star anise.

Return stock to stovetop and bring back to a boil. Slowly pour cornmeal into boiling stock, mixing vigorously with a whisk. When all cornmeal is well combined, lower the heat to simmer and continue to stir constantly with a wooden spoon. When polenta is thick and pulls away from the sides of the pot, after about 20 to 30 minutes, remove from heat. Add butter and mix until thoroughly combined.

Working quickly before it hardens, pour cooked polenta into the lined pan, cover with another sheet of plastic wrap, and pat it to a thickness of 1.25 cm (½″). Refrigerate until hard.

To bake, preheat the oven to 150° C (300° F).

Cut polenta into 1.25 × 7.5 cm (½ × 3″) frites. Dip in milk then roll in almonds. Set aside.

Pour a thin layer of oil into the bottom of a shallow frying pan. Heat on low to medium, and pan-fry frites until they are golden brown on all sides. Remove from oil with a slotted spoon and drain on a paper towel. Repeat until all frites are cooked. Transfer them to a wire rack and bake them in the oven for 5 minutes. Keep warm until serving time.

ORANGE-TARRAGON SAUCE
2 large egg yolks
30 mL (2 Tbsp) orange juice,
    page 151
zest of 1 orange
185 g (6.7 oz) clarified butter, melted
15 to 20 tarragon leaves, or to taste,
    chopped

Place egg yolks, juice and zest in a stainless steel bowl. Place the bowl over a saucepan of simmering but not boiling water on medium heat, and whisk until the mixture is thick and creamy. Remove from heat. Slowly stir in a very small amount of butter (too much will curdle the mixture), whisking constantly. Continue whisking and adding butter a little at a time so that it emulsifies and thickens. If emulsion is too thick, add a little more juice or water. Stir in tarragon. Keep warm until serving time.

CAMBOZOLA FONDANT
115 g (4.2 oz) Cambozola cheese, at
    room temperature
45 mL (3 Tbsp) whipping cream

Remove the outer rind from cheese. Discard. Cut cheese into cubes and place in a food processor. With the motor running, slowly pour in cream until the mixture is smooth and evenly blended. Refrigerate until needed, then form into 6 to 8 quenelles just before serving.

GARNISH

2 oranges, peeled, seeded and
    segmented
125 mL (½ cup) port reduction,
    page 153
6 to 8 sprigs fresh tarragon

ASSEMBLY

Place 3 frites side by side in the centre of each plate. Lay fondant across
frites and lean a pear steak against it.
Arrange an orange segment on either side of the frites. Spoon reduction in front. Garnish with a sprig of
tarragon. Serve with a small side
dish of sauce.

WINE

A late-bottled vintage (LBV) port or
Canadian VQA Cabernet Franc
icewine should pair well with the
pear and salty blue cheese flavours in
this dessert. A Sauternes would be
another suitable option.

Wheat berry pudding with candied black olives

WHEAT BERRIES are the whole unprocessed kernels of the wheat plant. In this dessert, their nutty flavour and firm consistency put a different spin on the traditional bread pudding. Combined with citrus-dressed strawberry carpaccio, candied black olives and lemon-mint emulsion, this earthy pudding is full of delicious surprises! Note that this is not a dessert to make in a hurry; the olives must marinate for 3 days. *Serves 8*

WHEAT BERRY PUDDING

75 g (2.7 oz) wheat berries
130 mL (½ cup + 1 tsp) frozen
    orange juice concentrate
2 large egg yolks
60 g (2.1 oz) granulated sugar
125 mL (½ cup) 2% milk
4 g (2) gelatin leaves, bloomed
20 g (0.7 oz) unsalted butter
30 g (1.1 oz) pistachios, shelled
40 g (1.4 oz) golden raisins

In a medium saucepan, bring 750 mL (3 cups) water to a boil. Add berries and cook, uncovered, until they are al dente. Drain, return berries to saucepan, add juice, and continue cooking over low heat until all liquid is absorbed. Remove from heat and set aside.

In a stainless steel bowl, combine egg yolks and sugar; whisk lightly until sugar is dissolved. Pour milk into the egg mixture a little at a time, whisking constantly. Place the bowl over a saucepan of simmering but not boiling water on medium heat, and whisk until the mixture reaches 85°C (185°F), or until the mixture coats the back of a spoon. Remove from heat and add gelatin. Combine with the cream mixture until completely dissolved.

Heat butter in a frying pan. Toss pistachios in butter to toast them, then sauté with raisins. Stir the nut-raisin mixture into wheat berries. Fold into the cream mixture. Refrigerate, allowing grains to absorb any excess liquid.

Spoon puddings into individual 5 cm (2″) metal ring moulds. Refrigerate until serving time.

CANDIED BLACK OLIVES

32 black olives, pitted and halved
300 g (10.8 oz) granulated sugar
200 mL (¾ cup + 1 Tbsp) water
zest of 1 orange
1 vanilla bean

Bring a small pot of water to a boil; blanch the olives and remove them with a slotted spoon. Discard boiled water. Bring another pot of water to a boil; blanch the olives again. Drain and set aside. (Blanch olives a third time if they are very salty.)

Combine sugar, water and zest in a saucepan. Split vanilla bean in half lengthwise, scrape out seeds, then add seeds and pod to the syrup mixture; bring to a boil. Add olives, reduce heat, and simmer for about 10 minutes. Cool, then refrigerate in an airtight container for 3 days. Remove olives from syrup with a slotted spoon and drain on a wire rack.

STRAWBERRY CARPACCIO

8 fresh strawberries, thinly sliced
citrus dressing, to taste, page 153

Toss strawberries with dressing just before serving.

GARNISH

8 scoops green apple–skin sorbet,
    page 154
125 mL (½ cup) mint emulsion,
    page 152

ASSEMBLY

Place a pudding in the centre of each plate. Top with 4 candied olive halves. Place a scoop of sorbet on pudding and top with carpaccio. Drizzle emulsion and syrup from confit around pudding. Serve immediately.

WINE

A Tokaji from Hungary, vin de paille, Sauternes or Sauterne-style wine from France should pair well with the orange and earthy/nutty flavours of the creamy grain pudding. Other options may include a Vin Santo or Asti Spumante.

cookies and chocolates

The grand finale

———— ❊ ————

To PROPERLY FINISH a meal, serve cookies (also called petits fours secs) and chocolates. More than just frivolous little morsels, these small fancy cookies and elaborate chocolate confections offer guests one last impressive taste. Each piece is precisely crafted and presented like a precious jewel to stimulate all the senses.

The cookies and chocolates featured in this chapter are similar in flavour to those we sell commercially in our collections of Wild Sweets chocolates and other confections. However, they are much simpler in presentation (see page 135 or visit our virtual boutique). With only one or two bites to make an impression, the flavour of these cookies and chocolates should be intense. Use the perfect, concentrated flavours of fresh spices, aromatic herbs, infused oils, caramelized nut paste and dried wild berries to boost the intensity of the cookies. For the chocolates, use the best-quality chocolate you can find; it will make all the difference. (See page 91 for information and recommendations about chocolate.)

Serve an assortment of both cookies and chocolates for a visually exciting presentation and texturally contrasting experience. Although these cookies and chocolates are traditionally served after a meal, they are wonderful as a special treat at any time and for any occasion. Pairing these little gems with the appropriate beverage will heighten the dining experience. Coffee or tea, of course, is a perfect choice. But so is a striking fortified sweet wine such as an Australian Liqueur Muscat or Liqueur Tokay, a French Banyuls, a tawny port from Portugal or a Vin Santo from Italy.

Note: All of the recipes in this section have been made and tested using a specific chocolate percentage. Ganaches, which are based on emulsification (page 65), are particularly susceptible to differences in cocoa and cocoa butter content; to ensure success, we recommend you use chocolate with the specified percentage in these recipes.

Cookies

SZECHWAN PEPPER COCOA BARKS

150 g (5.3 oz) cake flour

12 g (0.4 oz) unsweetened cocoa powder

125 g (4.5 oz) salted butter

50 g (1.9 oz) icing sugar

1 small egg

60 g (2.1 oz) roasted hazelnuts, coarsely chopped

2.5 mL (½ tsp) vanilla extract

7.5 mL (1½ tsp) Szechwan pepper, coarsely ground

Sift flour and cocoa together. Set aside.

Using an electric mixer with a paddle attachment, cream butter and sugar. Add egg, hazelnuts, vanilla and pepper. Mix on low speed until thoroughly combined. Add the cocoa mixture and mix on low speed until thoroughly combined. Do not overmix.

Place the dough on a silicone mat. Cover with another silicone mat and roll the dough to a thickness of about 5 mm (¼″). Refrigerate until set, about 2 hours (overnight is best).

To bake, preheat the oven to 150°C (300°F). Line a baking sheet with a silicone mat or silicone paper. Cut cookies into 2.5 × 5 cm (1 × 2″) rectangles or other desired shapes. Arrange cookies on the baking sheet, leaving at least 2 finger spaces between each cookie. Bake for 10 to 12 minutes, or until dark brown in colour. Remove from baking sheet and cool on a wire rack. Store in an airtight container. These cookies can also be frozen. Thaw in the fridge overnight.

Yield: 2½ dozen

GRAPEFRUIT AND BORAGE HONEY DENTELLES

40 g (1.4 oz) unsalted butter

120 g (4.3 oz) borage honey

50 g (1.9 oz) almonds, sliced

30 g (1.1 oz) all-purpose flour

45 mL (3 Tbsp) grapefruit juice, page 151

zest of ¼ grapefruit

5 mL (1 tsp) grapefruit oil, page 151

Melt butter in a large microwaveable bowl. Add honey, almonds, flour, juice, zest and oil, mixing well until thoroughly combined. Refrigerate for at least 2 hours in a plastic container with a tight-fitting lid (overnight is best).

To bake, preheat the oven to 200°C (400°F). Line a baking sheet with a silicone mat or paper. Drop the dough by teaspoonfuls onto the mat, leaving at least 7.5 cm (3″) around each dentelle. Bake for 6 to 8 minutes, or until golden brown. Remove from baking sheet, shape warm dentelles over a rolling pin, and cool briefly on a wire rack. Store in an airtight container.

Yield: 4 dozen

BUCKWHEAT HONEY GINGERSNAPS

90 g (3.2 oz) granulated sugar

25 g (0.9 oz) molasses

45 g (1.6 oz) buckwheat honey

45 g (1.6 oz) unsalted butter

pinch of ground ginger

pinch of ground cinnamon

1.25 mL (¼ tsp) baking soda

pinch of salt

40 mL (2 Tbsp + 2 tsp) water

135 g (4.8 oz) all-purpose flour

70 g (2.5 oz) buckwheat flour

36 whole natural almonds

Using an electric mixer with a paddle attachment, cream sugar, molasses, honey, butter, ginger, cinnamon, baking soda and salt. Add water and flours, and mix on low speed until thoroughly combined. The dough should hold. Do not overmix. Wrap the dough in plastic wrap and refrigerate for at least 2 hours (overnight is best).

To bake, preheat the oven to 165°C (325°F). Line a baking sheet with a silicone mat or silicone paper. Roll out dough on a lightly floured surface to a thickness of about 5 mm (¼″). Cut the dough into desired shapes and press an almond into the centre of each cookie. Arrange cookies on the baking sheet, leaving at least 1 finger space around each one, and bake for 5 to 7 minutes. Remove from the baking sheet and cool on a wire rack. Store in an airtight container. These cookies can also be frozen. Thaw in the fridge overnight.

Yield: 3 dozen

clockwise from brown rectangular cookie at top centre:
Szechwan pepper cocoa bark *(p. 134)*; Grapefruit and borage honey dentelle *(p. 134)*; Buckwheat honey
gingersnap *(p. 134)*; Lemon and mint oil sucrée *(p. 137)*; Wattle seed and walnut wedge *(p. 137)*;
Tamarind and pumpkin seed sablé *(p. 137)*; Orange blossom and fennel financier *(p. 138)*; Anise and chickpea biscotti *(p. 138)*;
Coriander and orange oil gaufrette *(p. 138)*; *centre:* Sunflower and ginseng macaroon *(p. 139)*

LEMON AND MINT OIL SUCRÉES

2 large egg yolks, hard boiled
150 g (5.3 oz) unsalted butter
75 g (2.7 oz) icing sugar
zest of ½ lemon
3.75 mL (¾ tsp) mint oil, page 151
150 g (5.3 oz) cake flour

Finely grate egg yolks using a box grater.

Using an electric mixer fitted with a paddle attachment, cream egg yolk, butter, sugar, zest and oil. With the motor running at low speed, add flour and mix until thoroughly combined. Do not overmix. Wrap the dough in plastic wrap and refrigerate for several hours (overnight is best).

To bake, preheat the oven to 180°C (350°F). Line a baking sheet with a silicone mat or silicone paper. Roll the dough on a lightly floured surface to a thickness of about 5 mm (¼"). Cut the dough into desired shapes. Arrange cookies on the baking sheet, leaving at least 2 finger spaces around each one, and bake for 8 to 10 minutes, or until light golden brown. Remove from baking sheet and cool on a wire rack. Store in an airtight container. These cookies can also be frozen. Thaw in the fridge overnight.

Yield: 2½ dozen

WATTLE SEED AND WALNUT WEDGES

100 g (3.6 oz) salted butter
100 g (3.6 oz) icing sugar, sifted
10 g (0.4 oz) ground wattle seeds
    (available in specialty food stores,
    or substitute ground coffee)
1 small egg yolk
100 g (3.6 oz) walnuts, finely ground
135 g (4.8 oz) cake flour, sifted
1 large egg, beaten, for egg wash
walnut quarters for décor

Using an electric mixer with a paddle attachment, cream butter and sugar. Add seeds, egg yolk and walnuts, and mix until thoroughly combined. With the motor running at low speed, add flour and mix until thoroughly combined. Do not overmix. Wrap dough in plastic wrap and refrigerate at least 2 hours (overnight is best).

To bake, preheat the oven to 180°C (350°F). Line a baking sheet with a silicone mat or silicone paper. Roll out dough on a lightly floured surface to a thickness of about 5 mm (¼"). Cut dough into 5 cm (2") wide strips then into 3.75 cm (1½") triangles. Brush each wedge with some egg wash and garnish with a walnut quarter. Arrange cookies on the baking sheet and bake for 8 to 10 minutes, or until golden brown. Remove from baking sheet and cool on a wire rack. Store in an airtight container.

These cookies can also be frozen. Thaw in the fridge overnight.

Yield: 2½ dozen

TAMARIND AND PUMPKIN SEED SABLÉS

30 g (1.1 oz) tamarind paste
30 mL (1 Tbsp) hot water
180 g (6.4 oz) unsalted butter
25 g (0.9 oz) icing sugar
1 large egg
30 g (1.1 oz) dried apricots, finely
    chopped
60 g (2.1 oz) pumpkin seeds, finely
    chopped
240 g (8.6 oz) cake flour, sifted
1 egg white, beaten, for egg wash
10 g (0.4 oz) pumpkin seeds for décor
60 g (2.1 oz) granulated sugar for
    décor

Rehydrate tamarind paste in hot water. Allow to stand for 10 minutes, then strain liquid and reserve. Discard any solids.

Using an electric mixer with a paddle attachment, cream tamarind liquid, butter and icing sugar. Add egg and continue mixing until thoroughly combined. Fold in apricots and 60 g (2.1 oz) seeds by hand with a rubber spatula, then fold in flour. Wrap the dough in plastic wrap and refrigerate for at least 1 hour (overnight is best).

To bake, preheat the oven to 180°C (350°F). Line a baking sheet with a silicone mat or silicone paper. Roll the dough on a lightly floured surface to a thickness of about 5 mm (¼"). Cut the dough into desired shapes. Brush each cookie with some egg wash, press a few seeds into the dough, and cover completely with sprinkled sugar. Arrange cookies on the baking sheet and bake for 8 to 10 minutes. Remove from the baking sheet and cool on a wire rack. Store in an airtight container. These cookies can also be frozen. Thaw in the fridge overnight.

Yield: 4 dozen

ORANGE BLOSSOM AND FENNEL FINANCIERS

125 g (4.5 oz) icing sugar

50 g (1.9 oz) all-purpose flour

2.5 mL (½ tsp) baking powder

75 g (2.7 oz) almonds, finely ground

15 mL (1 Tbsp) fennel seeds, coarsely ground

150 g (5.3 oz) egg whites (about 5 large)

2.5 mL (½ tsp) orange blossom water, or to taste

zest of 1 orange

130 g (4.6 oz) salted butter

Preheat the oven to 150°C (300°F).

Sift sugar, flour and baking powder into a large bowl. Add almonds, fennel seeds, egg whites, orange blossom water and zest, whisking well until all ingredients are thoroughly combined.

Make a brown butter by cooking butter in a heavy saucepan over low heat. When butter starts to foam, milk solids at the bottom of the pan start to turn brown (but are not burned), and the mixture has a pleasant nutty odour, remove from heat. Slowly pour over the fennel mixture a little bit at a time, whisking constantly until all ingredients are thoroughly incorporated.

Pipe or spoon the mixture into 5 cm (2″) flexible silicone moulds or nonstick muffin tins. Bake for 12 to 14 minutes, or until a toothpick inserted in the centre of the cookie comes out clean. Unmould and cool on a wire rack. Store in an airtight container. These cookies may also be frozen. Thaw in the fridge overnight then heat slowly in a warm oven for a few minutes before serving.

Yield: 3 dozen

ANISE AND CHICKPEA BISCOTTI

175 g (6.3 oz) pastry flour

40 g (1.4 oz) chickpea flour

5 g (0.25 oz) baking powder

1½ large eggs (or 2 medium)

140 g (5 oz) granulated sugar

2.5 mL (½ tsp) salt

2.5 mL (½ tsp) vanilla extract

2.5 mL (½ tsp) orange oil, page 151

zest of ½ orange

7.5 mL (1½ tsp) anise powder

75 g (2.7 oz) whole natural hazelnuts

Preheat the oven to 165°C (325°F). Line a 15 × 20 cm (6 × 8″) nonstick pan with silicone paper.

Sift flours and baking powder together. Set aside.

Using an electric mixer with a paddle attachment, cream eggs, sugar, salt, vanilla, oil, zest and anise powder. Add the flour mixture and mix on low speed until thoroughly combined. Do not overmix. Fold in hazelnuts by hand with a rubber spatula.

Press dough evenly into the pan. Bake for 30 to 40 minutes, or until golden brown. Unmould onto a wire rack and cool.

Reduce oven to 135°C (275°F). Using a sharp serrated knife, cut the loaf into long 5 cm (2″) wide strips. Then cut each strip into 15 mm (½″) thick bars. Lay all cookies flat on a baking sheet and bake until toasted and dry, about 20 to 30 minutes. Cool on a wire rack. Store in an airtight container.

Note: These cookies can also be frozen after the first baking. (Cut the loaf into cookies before freezing.) Thaw in the fridge overnight and bake a second time as directed.

Yield: 4 dozen

CORIANDER AND ORANGE OIL GAUFRETTES

125 g (4.5 oz) icing sugar

40 g (1.4 oz) all-purpose flour

2.5 mL (½ tsp) ground coriander

65 g (2.4 oz) egg whites (about 2 large)

40 g (1.4 oz) unsalted butter, melted

2.5 mL (½ tsp) orange oil, page 151

Sift sugar, flour and coriander into a large bowl. Slowly add egg whites, whisking constantly until well combined. In a small bowl, combine butter and oil. Mix into the dough until thoroughly combined. Transfer the dough to a plastic container with a tight-fitting lid and refrigerate for at least 1 hour (overnight is best).

To bake, preheat the oven to 180°C (350°F). Line a baking sheet with a silicone mat or silicone paper.

Draw a 7.5 × 15 cm (3 × 6″) rectangle onto the lid of a plastic container. Cut out the rectangle, leaving a plastic stencil. Place the stencil on a silicone mat, and spread the dough evenly to a thickness of 1.5 mm (1/16″) over the hollow of the stencil using an offset spatula. Repeat, placing no more than 2 cookies per baking sheet (these cookies cool quickly so bake only 2 cookies at a time or they will become too brittle to roll). Bake for about 4 minutes, or until light golden brown. Remove from baking sheet and wrap around a 2.5 cm (1″) wooden dowel. Roll cookies loosely; they are very fragile and rolling them too tightly will cause them to break when you remove them from the dowel. Cool on a wire rack and store in an airtight container.

Yield: 3 dozen

SUNFLOWER AND GINSENG MACAROONS

225 g (8.1 oz) icing sugar, sifted
50 g (1.9 oz) sunflower seeds, shelled
75 g (2.7 oz) whole almonds, shelled
5 mL (1 tsp) pure ginseng tea powder
100 g (3.6 oz) egg whites (about
    3 large)
25 g (0.9 oz) granulated sugar
lemon oil, page 151, to taste

Note: This recipe makes 4 dozen cookies. Do not try to make less than this; it will be hard to whip smaller amounts of egg whites.

Preheat the oven to 180°C (350°F). Grind sugar, seeds, almonds and ginseng in a food processor. Set aside.

Using an electric mixer fitted with a whisk, beat egg whites for a few seconds on high speed. Reduce to medium speed. As soon as foam starts to slide from the sides of the bowl and no longer gains volume, turn mixer to maximum speed. With the motor running, add sugar slowly, continuing to whip until egg whites form stiff peaks.

Just before baking, use a rubber spatula to gently fold egg whites and lemon oil into the almond mixture until all ingredients are thoroughly combined. Spoon the batter into a piping bag fitted with a plain round tube. Pipe into 2.5 cm (1″) mounds on silicone paper. Leave at least 2 finger spaces between each macaroon. Place on a baking sheet and bake for 8 to 10 minutes, or until golden brown.

Remove the cookies from the oven. Pour a thin layer of cold water between the paper and the baking sheet to create steam under macaroons. Allow to cool slightly, then transfer cookies from the paper to a wire rack and cool completely. Store in an airtight container.

Yield: 4 dozen

creaming

Creaming is the operation of manually or mechanically mixing two (or more) ingredients—fat and sugar—until the mixture is smooth and "creamy." In this homogeneous mixture, sugar grains suspended within fat molecules trap air around them. These air pockets act as the leavening agent during baking.

Butter (sweet or salty) is typically used as the fat because shortenings have already been aerated and oils (liquid fats) will not incorporate air. Butter is also an anti-staling agent (it keeps baked products fresher longer) and it prevents the starch granules in flour from clumping when a liquid is added.

Separation, or unmixed particles, is the most common failure in the creaming process. Here are some tips for preventing separation:

ROOM TEMPERATURE. The butter and other ingredients should be at room temperature, between 18°C (65°F) and 21°C (70°F), before mixing.

MECHANICAL MIXING. Electric mixers and food processors provide the best results because they aerate the mixture better than mixing by hand. Factors such as the amount of mixture, size of bowl, speed and type of mixer and the temperature of the room will affect the mixing time. We suggest a minimum of 4 and a maximum of 10 minutes.

PROPER METHOD. Fully cream the base mixture so that it is pale in colour, light and airy before incorporating any other ingredients. Add the eggs one at a time, fully incorporating each one before the next is added. Mixing in the eggs provides lecithin, the emulsifier from the yolk, and increases the amount of air in the batter. Add the dry and liquid ingredients alternately. Start with some liquid and finish with some dry—adding flour last ensures that all of the liquid is absorbed.

Back to front, left to right:

1. Carrot and cardamom truffles *(p. 143)*; 2. Canadian maple whisky truffles *(p. 143)*;

3. Chokeberry and kriek pavés *(p. 144)*; 4. Wild blueberry and lavender pavés *(p. 144)*; 5. Cashew and Brazil nut harlequins *(p. 148)*;

6. Corn, walnut and malt croquants *(p. 149)*; 7. Fruit and crystallized herb mendiants *(p.144)*; 8. Blood orange and

fleur de sel pavés *(p.145)*; 9. Celery and walnut croustillant chocolates *(p. 148)*; 10. Alpine strawberry and basil pavés *(p.149)*

Chocolates

CARROT AND CARDAMOM TRUFFLES

GANACHE

260 g (9.3 oz) milk chocolate

85 g (3.1 oz) 70% cocoa dark chocolate

130 mL (½ cup + 1 tsp) carrot juice

18 g (0.6 oz) clover honey

18 g (0.6 oz) corn syrup

45 g (1.6 oz) salted butter, softened

Line the bottom and sides of a 20 cm (8″) square pan with plastic wrap.

Fill a medium saucepan with 5 cm (2″) water and bring to a boil. Turn off the heat but leave the pot on the burner. Combine chocolates in a stainless steel bowl; place the bowl over the pan of hot water for the mixture to melt. Set aside.

Combine juice, honey and syrup in a saucepan; bring to a boil. Pour the syrup mixture over the melted chocolate, stirring from the centre in a circular motion with a wooden spoon or rubber spatula to emulsify the ganache. Stir until all ingredients are combined but try not to incorporate any air. Fold in butter. Pour the ganache into the pan to a thickness of 1.25 cm (½″). Allow to rest at room temperature until ganache is firm, about 24 to 48 hours.

Line a baking sheet with silicone paper. With a warm dry knife, cut the ganache into 2.5 cm (1″) squares. Lay them on the baking sheet, leaving space around each ganache. Allow to stand at room temperature to firm for at least a couple of hours, 1 day is best.

GARNISH

250 g (9.1 oz) graham cracker crumbs

10 mL (2 tsp) ground cardamom, or to taste

500 g (18.2 oz) milk chocolate, tempered

ASSEMBLY

Combine crumbs with cardamom; set on a baking sheet. Using a chocolate dipping fork or a regular dinner fork, dip the squares in tempered chocolate. Remove excess chocolate that drips at the base of the fork. Slide the chocolate onto the crumbs. With another fork, completely cover the wet chocolate with crumbs by sprinkling crumbs over the chocolate. Do not move the chocolate until it sets completely, about 3 to 5 minutes. Shake off excess crumbs and set chocolate aside. (Dipping and sprinkling is easier with 2 people.) Repeat until all chocolates are dipped and coated. Store in an airtight container in a cool, dry place but do not refrigerate.

Yield: 4 dozen

CANADIAN MAPLE WHISKY TRUFFLES

GANACHE

150 mL (½ cup + 2 Tbsp) whipping cream

20 g (0.7 oz) borage honey

20 g (0.7 oz) corn syrup

250 g (9.1 oz) 70% cocoa dark chocolate, finely chopped

65 g (2.4 oz) salted butter, softened

45 mL (3 Tbsp) Canadian maple whisky (or liqueur)

Line the bottom and sides of a 20 cm (8″) square pan with plastic wrap.

Combine cream, honey and syrup in a saucepan; bring to a boil. Place chocolate in a bowl. Pour the cream mixture over chocolate, stirring from the centre in a circular motion with a wooden spoon or rubber spatula to emulsify the ganache. Stir until all ingredients are combined but try not to incorporate any air. Fold in butter and whisky. Pour the ganache into the pan to a thickness of 1.25 cm (½″). Allow to rest at room temperature until ganache is firm, about 24 to 48 hours.

Line a baking sheet with silicone paper. With a warm dry knife, cut the ganache into 2.5 cm (1″) squares. Lay them on the baking sheet, leaving space around each ganache. Allow to stand at room temperature to firm for at least a couple of hours, 1 day is best.

GARNISH

250 g (9.1 oz) unsweetened cocoa powder

500 g (18.2 oz) 70% cocoa dark chocolate, tempered

ASSEMBLY

Sift cocoa onto a baking sheet. Using a chocolate dipping fork or a regular dinner fork, dip the squares in tempered chocolate. Remove excess chocolate that drips at the base of the fork. Slide the chocolate onto the cocoa. With another fork, completely cover the wet chocolate with cocoa by sprinkling cocoa over the chocolate. Do not move the chocolate until it sets completely, about

3 to 5 minutes. Shake off excess cocoa and set chocolate aside. (Dipping and sprinkling is easier with 2 people.) Repeat until all chocolates are dipped. Store in an airtight container in a cool, dry place but do not refrigerate.

Yield: 4 dozen

CHOKECHERRY AND KRIEK PAVÉS
GANACHE

105 mL (⅓ cup + 1 Tbsp + 1 tsp)
   whipping cream
15 g (0.5 oz) wildflower honey
15 g (0.5 oz) corn syrup
210 g (7.6 oz) 70% cocoa dark chocolate, finely chopped
55 g (2 oz) salted butter, softened
85 mL (⅓ cup + 1 tsp) kriek beer

Combine cream, honey and syrup in a saucepan; bring to a boil. Place chocolate in a bowl. Pour the cream mixture over chocolate, stirring from the centre in a circular motion with a wooden spoon or rubber spatula to emulsify the ganache. Stir until all ingredients are combined but try not to incorporate any air. Fold in butter and kriek. Cool until the ganache has the consistency of soft butter.

GARNISH

ninety-six 2.5 cm (1″) squares 70%
   cocoa dark chocolate
12 dried chokecherries, finely diced
gold flakes (optional) (available from
   fine baking and/or graphic design
   suppliers)

ASSEMBLY

Spoon the ganache into a piping bag fitted with a plain round tube (or a star tube). Pipe a small mound of ganache onto the centre of a chocolate square. Top with a second square. Garnish with a few small cubes of chokecherry. Dust with gold flakes. Store in an airtight container in a cool, dry place but do not refrigerate.

Yield: 4 dozen

FRUIT AND CRYSTALLIZED HERB MENDIANTS

290 g (10.4 oz) white chocolate,
   tempered
48 dried cranberries
48 dried blueberries
12 dried apricots, cut in quarters
96 pumpkin seeds, toasted
48 crystallized mint leaves, page 156

Spoon the chocolate into a piping bag fitted with a plain round tube. Pipe a small circle of chocolate onto a silicone mat or a plastic (clear acetate) sheet. Immediately press a piece of each fruit, 2 seeds and a mint leaf into chocolate. Repeat until fruit, seeds, leaves and chocolate have been used. Store in an airtight container in a cool, dry place until needed but do not refrigerate.

Yield: 4 dozen

WILD BLUEBERRY AND LAVENDER-INFUSED PAVÉS
BLUEBERRY-LAVENDER INFUSION

165 mL (⅔ cup + 1 tsp) water
3.75 mL (¾ tsp) dried lavender,
   or to taste
100 g (3.6 oz) dried wild blueberries

Combine water and lavender in a saucepan; bring to a boil. Remove from heat, cover tightly with plastic wrap to create a natural vacuum, and allow flavours to infuse for at least 15 minutes.

Strain infusion and discard lavender. Add blueberries and bring water back to a boil for 2 to 3 minutes. Remove from heat, transfer to a plastic container with a lid, and allow to stand overnight. Just before serving, drain briefly on a paper towel.

GANACHE

180 mL (¾ cup) whipping cream
7.5 mL (1½ tsp) dried lavender
40 g (1.4 oz) borage honey
230 g (8.3 oz) 70% cocoa dark chocolate, finely chopped
25 g (0.9 oz) salted butter, softened

Combine cream and lavender in a saucepan; bring to a boil. Remove from heat, cover tightly with plastic wrap to create a natural vacuum, and allow flavours to infuse for at least 30 minutes.

Strain cream and discard lavender. Add honey and bring cream back to a boil.

Place chocolate in a bowl. Pour the cream mixture over chocolate, stirring from the centre in a circular motion with a wooden spoon or rubber spatula to emulsify the ganache. Stir until all ingredients are combined but try not to incorporate any air. Fold in butter. Cool until the ganache has the consistency of soft butter.

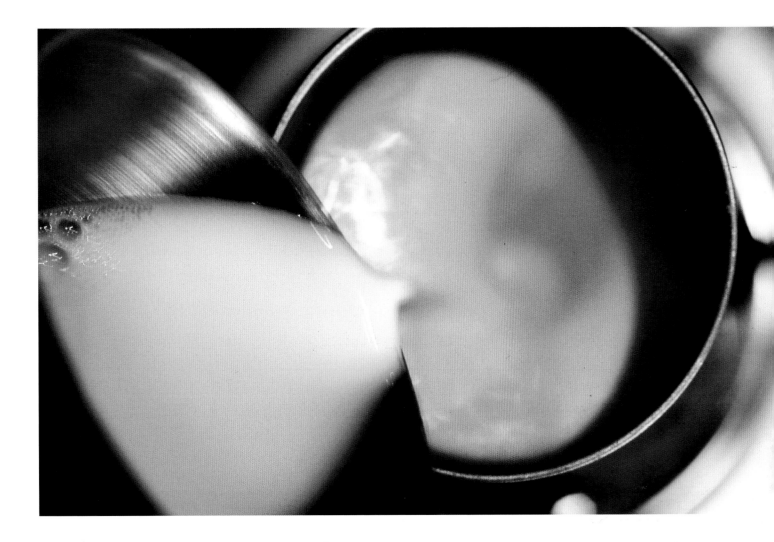

BLUEBERRY POWDER (OPTIONAL)

125 g (4.5 oz) fresh or frozen
   blueberries

Preheat the oven to 60°C (125°F).

Using a juicing machine, process
blueberries. Reserve pulp and freeze
juice for later use. Spread pulp on a
silicone mat and dry in the oven for
30 to 45 minutes. (You can also place
the pulp in a microwaveable dish and
dry in a microwave oven on high,
in 20- to 30- second intervals. As
blueberries begin to dry, cook for
shorter and shorter intervals.)

Pulse dry pulp in a coffee grinder
until it becomes a fine powder. (You
may need to pass it through a fine-
mesh sieve and grind it several
times.) Store in an airtight container.

GARNISH

ninety-six 2.5 cm (1″) squares white
   chocolate

96 dried wild blueberries

gold flakes (optional) (available from
   fine baking and/or graphic design
   suppliers)

ASSEMBLY

Spoon the ganache into a piping
bag fitted with a plain round tube (or
a star tube). Pipe a small mound of
ganache onto the centre of a chocolate square. Press an infused blueberry in the centre of the ganache.
Top with a second square. Garnish
with 2 dried blueberries. Dust with
gold flakes and blueberry powder.
Store in an airtight container in a
cool, dry place but do not refrigerate.

Yield: 4 dozen

BLOOD ORANGE AND

FLEUR DE SEL PAVÉS

GANACHE

80 mL (⅓ cup) whipping cream

80 mL (⅓ cup) blood orange juice,
   page 151

15 g (0.6 oz) granulated sugar

16 g (0.6 oz) corn syrup

15 mL (1 Tbsp) water

50 g (1.9 oz) milk chocolate, finely
   chopped

180 g (6.4 oz) 70% cocoa dark chocolate, finely chopped

20 g (0.7 oz) salted butter, softened

30 mL (2 Tbsp) curaçao, or to taste

Combine cream and juice in a
small saucepan; heat to body temperature and set aside.

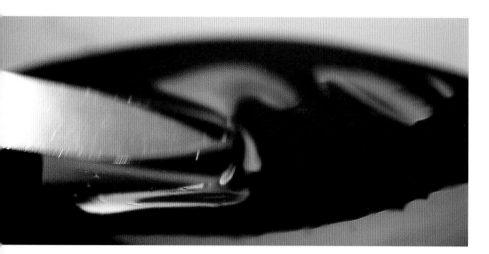

tempering

Tempering is the operation of stabilizing a chocolate mass through melting and cooling at specific temperatures until the right crystals are formed. Tempering involves three temperature stages. First, the chocolate is heated to 45°C (113°F) so that all existing cocoa butter crystals are melted. Then, it is cooled to between 27°C (81°F) and 29°C (85°F) so that different cocoa butter crystals can form and grow. The chocolate is stirred for at least 5 minutes so it becomes thicker and more viscous. Finally, the chocolate is warmed to between 29°C (85°F) and 32°C (90°F) to stabilize the crystals, making the chocolate fluid and ready to use.

Chocolate is usually tempered using one of two methods. For the *table method,* heat the chocolate to 45°C (113°F) and pour half of it on a clean, dry marble or stainless steel slab. Using a spatula, quickly move the mixture back and forth on the cool surface until it thickens and becomes corn syrupy–like in consistency. Quickly scrape it back into the remaining half and stir for at least 5 minutes. Repeat with a smaller amount if it is not at the right temperature. For the *microwave method,* or *injection method,* heat two-thirds of the chocolate to 45°C (113°F), then finely chop the remaining third and add it to the melted mixture. Stir until the mixture is smooth, homogenous and at the optimum temperature. Successfully tempered and set chocolate will shine, snap and contract. Note that water is chocolate's number one enemy. Even the smallest drop can seize the chocolate mass, so ensure that all utensils and surfaces are completely free of moisture when tempering.

The optimum temperature for the 3 types of chocolate at each stage of the tempering process is:

	STAGE 1	STAGE 2	STAGE 3
White	45°C (113°F)	27°C (81°C)	29°C (85°F)
Milk	45°C (113°F)	28°C (83°F)	30°C (86°F)
Dark	45°C (113°F)	29°C (85°F)	32°C (90°F)

Tempered chocolate can be poured into moulds or used to dip or coat fillings then very briefly cooled in the fridge. Finished products should be stored in a cool, dry place with a constant temperature no higher than 20°C (68°F).

Combine sugar, syrup and water in another saucepan; cook over high heat until the mixture is caramel in colour. Remove from heat and de-cook with the cream mixture.

Place chocolates in a bowl. Strain the cream mixture over chocolate, stirring from the centre in a circular motion with a wooden spoon or rubber spatula to emulsify the ganache. Stir until all ingredients are combined but try not to incorporate any air. Fold in butter and curaçao. Cool until the ganache has the consistency of soft butter.

CANDIED ORANGE ZESTS
50 g (1.9 oz) granulated sugar
50 mL (3 Tbsp + 1 tsp) water
zest of 1 orange (peel the orange
    leaving the zest in large strips,
    then remove as much of the
    pith as possible)
Combine sugar and water in a saucepan; bring to a boil. Add zest and simmer over low heat for about 1 hour. Transfer to an airtight container. Refrigerate overnight. Remove pieces of white pith from zests and discard. Pat zests dry and cut into small julienne strips.

GARNISH
ninety-six 2.5 cm (1″) squares 70%
    cocoa dark chocolate
6 g (0.3 oz) fleur de sel

ASSEMBLY
Spoon the ganache into a piping bag fitted with a plain round tube (or a star tube). Pipe a small mound of ganache onto the centre of a chocolate square. Top with a second square. Garnish with a few strands

of zest and sprinkle with fleur de sel. Store in an airtight container in a cool, dry place but do not refrigerate.
Yield: 4 dozen

CASHEW AND BRAZIL NUT HARLEQUINS
CASHEW MIXTURE
100 g (3.6 oz) cashew nuts, toasted
100 g (3.6 oz) icing sugar
100 g (3.6 oz) milk chocolate, melted
45 mL (3 Tbsp) grapeseed oil
90 g (3.2 oz) cashew praline,
    page 156

BRAZIL NUT MIXTURE
100 g (3.6 oz) Brazil nuts, toasted
100 g (3.6 oz) icing sugar
100 g (3.6 oz) 70% cocoa dark choco-
    late, melted
45 mL (3 Tbsp) grapeseed oil
90 g (3.2 oz) Brazil nut praline,
    page 156
In a food processor, grind cashews and sugar. With the motor running, add chocolate, oil and praline. The mixture should have the consistency of mayonnaise. Set aside. Repeat using Brazil nuts.

To make the chocolates pictured here, you will need to spread layers of each mixture, as evenly as possible, on top of each other, making sure that each layer has hardened before you spread on the next. In our atelier, we use special chocolate frames in sizes of 0.5 cm, 1.25 cm, 1.5 cm and 2.5 cm (¼″, ½″, ¾″ and 1″). If you do not have frames, line a 12.5 × 22.5 cm (5 × 9″) loaf pan with silicone paper. Spread ½ the cashew mixture as evenly as possible into the pan to a depth of about 0. 5 cm (¼″).

Allow to set until hard, about 20 to 30 minutes. Spread a layer of Brazil nut mixture on top. Allow to set until hard. Repeat with the remaining cashew mixture. Finish with the remaining Brazil nut mixture. Allow the entire nut filling to set until hard, about 20 to 30 minutes. With a sharp knife or a cookie cutter, cut the nut filling into 2.5 cm (1″) round or square pieces.

GARNISH
500 g (18.2 oz) 70% cocoa dark
    chocolate, tempered
gold flakes (optional)
Dip the bottom of each square or round in chocolate, leaving the top ½ undipped. Set chocolate-side down on a silicone mat or paper to harden. Garnish with gold flakes. Store in airtight container in a cool, dry place but do not refrigerate.
Yield: 3¾ dozen

CELERY AND WALNUT CROUSTILLANT CHOCOLATES
GANACHE
165 mL (⅔ cup + 1 tsp) whipping
    cream
35 mL (2 Tbsp + 1 tsp) celery juice
zest of 1 lemon, very finely grated
    (use a rasp)
75 g (2.7 oz) 70% cocoa dark choco-
    late, finely chopped
165 g (5.9 oz) milk chocolate, finely
    chopped
60 g (2.1 oz) salted butter, softened
Combine cream, juice and zest in a saucepan; bring to a boil. (Strain cream and discard zest if it was not

grated with a rasp.) Place chocolates in a bowl. Pour the cream mixture over chocolate, stirring from the centre in a circular motion with a wooden spoon or rubber spatula to emulsify the ganache. Stir until all ingredients are combined but try not to incorporate any air. Fold in butter. Cool until the ganache has the consistency of soft butter.

GARNISH

96 celery seed and walnut croustillants, page 156, cut into 2.5 cm (1″) rounds and baked in 2.5 cm (1″) round flexible silicone moulds
48 crystallized celery leaves, page 156

ASSEMBLY

Spoon the ganache into a piping bag fitted with a plain round tube (or a star tube). Pipe a small mound of ganache onto the centre of a croustillant. Top with a second croustillant. Garnish with a celery leaf. Store in an airtight container in a cool, dry place but do not refrigerate.

Yield: 4 dozen

CORN, WALNUT AND MALT CROQUANTS

CROQUANT

200 g (7.2 oz) milk chocolate
30 g (1.1 oz) salted butter
160 g (5.7 oz) walnut praline, page 156
100 g (3.6 oz) corn flakes
10 mL (2 tsp) malt powder

Line a 12.5 × 22.5 cm (5 × 9″) loaf pan with plastic wrap.

Fill a medium saucepan with 5 cm (2″) water and bring to a boil. Turn

off the heat but leave the pot on the burner. Combine chocolate and butter in a stainless steel bowl; place the bowl over the pan of hot water for the mixture to melt. Make sure that the mixture is no warmer than body temperature. Remove from heat and stir in praline, corn flakes and malt powder. Pour the mixture into the pan, pressing it evenly. Allow to set about 1 hour and cut, with a serrated knife, into 2.5 cm (1″) squares.

GARNISH

sixty-eight 2.5 cm (1″) squares 70% cocoa dark chocolate
45 corn flakes

Set a square of croquant onto the centre of a chocolate square. Cut a second chocolate square in half on the diagonal. Top the croquant with a chocolate triangle. Garnish with a corn flake. Store in an airtight container in a cool, dry place but do not refrigerate.

Yield: 3¾ dozen

ALPINE STRAWBERRY AND BASIL-INFUSED PAVÉS

BASIL INFUSION

25 mL (1 Tbsp + 2 tsp) water
1 g (0.05 oz) fresh basil leaves (about 5 large leaves)

Combine water and basil in a saucepan; bring to a boil. Remove from heat, cover tightly with plastic wrap to create a natural vacuum, and allow flavours to infuse for 30 minutes. Strain and discard basil. Set aside.

GANACHE

15 mL (1 Tbsp) basil infusion
15 g (0.5 oz) corn syrup
125 mL (½ cup) alpine strawberry purée, page 151
15 g (0.5 oz) wildflower honey
85 g (3.1 oz) 70% cocoa dark chocolate, finely chopped
165 g (5.9 oz) milk chocolate, finely chopped
40 g (1.4 oz) salted butter, softened

Combine infusion, syrup, purée and honey in a saucepan; bring to a boil. Place chocolates in a bowl. Pour the purée mixture over chocolate, stirring from the centre in a circular motion with a wooden spoon or rubber spatula to emulsify the ganache. Stir until all ingredients are combined but try not to incorporate any air. Fold in butter. Cool until the ganache has the consistency of soft butter.

GARNISH

ninety-six 2.5 cm (1″) white chocolate squares
48 fresh or dried alpine strawberries
red sugar granules (optional)

ASSEMBLY

Spoon the ganache into a piping bag fitted with a plain round tube (or a star tube). Pipe a small mound of ganache onto the centre of a chocolate square. Top with a second square. Garnish with a strawberry. Sprinkle with red sugar granules. Store in an airtight container in a cool, dry place but do not refrigerate.

Yield: 4 dozen

the basics

Fruit juice and purée

In this book, all fruit juices (except for the juice of citrus fruit such as lemons and oranges) are referred to as purée, a professional pastry term for a commercially processed fruit. Purées can easily be made at home using a fruit juicer (follow individual machine operating instructions). We suggest you use organic fruit.

BASIC METHOD

For fruit with edible peels (tree fruit such as apples and pears), thoroughly wash the skin. Cut fruit into quarters. Remove any large stones, but small pits, seeds, skin and stems can be puréed. For fruit with inedible peels (melons and citrus fruit), remove the skin.

Purée in a fruit juicer, following the operating instructions for the machine. Use the resulting purée as is, or sweeten lightly with corn syrup (up to 10%) if you wish to freeze the purée. Frozen purée can be stored up to 1 year.

Fruit stock

2 L (8 cups) water
50 g (1.9 oz) granulated sugar
zest and juice of 1 medium lemon
zest and juice of 1 medium orange
1 medium apple, cut in 2.5 cm
   (1″) dice
1 medium pear, cut in 2.5 cm
   (1″) dice

1 large carrot, cut in 2.5 cm (1″) dice
1 star anise
1 stick licorice root

Combine water, sugar, lemon zest and lemon juice in a large saucepan; bring to a boil. Add orange zest, orange juice, apple, pear, carrot, star anise and licorice. Reduce heat to low and simmer for about 30 minutes.

Strain the mixture through cheesecloth, making sure not to press or crush the fruit. Cool and refrigerate the stock for several days or freeze for up to 6 months.

Note: Press the strained fruit through a fine-mesh strainer or a tamis. The resulting purée can be used as an alternative to cream or butter in low-fat desserts.

Yield: 2 L (8 cups)

Infused oils

HERB OIL

100 g (3.6 oz) herb, washed
250 mL (1 cup) grapeseed oil
pinch of ascorbic acid (see note)

Note: Look for ascorbic acid in health food stores where you will find it in powder form or as vitamin C pills, which can be ground to a powder. Ascorbic acid is an antioxidant and naturally prevents herbs from turning brown when exposed to air.

Bring water to a boil in a small saucepan. Blanch herbs in boiling water for a few seconds, then plunge them immediately into an ice-water bath to stop the cooking. Drain herbs, squeezing out any excess water, then place them in a high-speed blender. Add oil and acid and blend for 3 to 4 minutes, until all the chlorophyll is released and the mixture is green. Transfer to a clean container, refrigerate, and allow to infuse overnight.

Strain oil through cheesecloth. Discard herbs. Refrigerate oil another 24 hours so that any impurities will separate. Pour clear oil into an airtight container, being careful to discard any sediment that may have settled out. Refrigerate until needed, or up to 7 days.

Yield: 180 mL (¾ cup)

CITRUS OIL

zest of 1 citrus fruit, preferably
   organic
60 mL (¼ cup) grapeseed oil

Wash fruit. Remove zest from fruit using a rasp. Place zest and oil in a high-speed blender and blend for 3 to 4 minutes. Transfer to a clean container, refrigerate, and allow to infuse overnight.

Strain oil through cheesecloth. Discard zest. Refrigerate oil another 24 hours so that any impurities will separate. Pour clear oil into an airtight container, being careful to discard any sediment that may have settled out. Refrigerate until needed, or up to 7 days.

Note: For a more intense flavour, add a few drops of high-quality flavoured oil extract, which is available in aromatherapy stores. Ask your salesperson for advice on which oils are edible.

Yield: 50 mL (3 Tbsp + 1 tsp)

Simple syrup

250 mL (1 cup) water
250 g (9.1 oz) granulated sugar

Combine water and sugar in a saucepan; bring to a boil. Remove from heat immediately. (If boiled longer, syrup will become sweeter as water evaporates.) Pour syrup into a clean plastic container with a tight-fitting lid. Seal the container immediately to trap in steam and protect against recrystallization. Cool then refrigerate until needed. This syrup will keep refrigerated for several weeks.

Yield: 500 mL (2 cups)

Emulsions

An emulsion mixes two liquids which would not ordinarily combine smoothly; for example, oil and water. By adding one liquid slowly to the other and mixing at high speed, the droplets disperse and seem to combine.

HERB EMULSION

75 g (2.7 oz) granulated sugar
5 mL (1 tsp) powdered pectin
75 mL (¼ cup 1 Tbsp) water
50 g (1.9 oz) herb(s)
45 mL (3 Tbsp) grapeseed oil
pinch of ascorbic acid (see note)

Note: Look for ascorbic acid in health food stores where you will find it in powder form or as vitamin C pills, which can be ground to a powder. Ascorbic acid is an antioxidant and naturally prevents herbs from turning brown when exposed to air.

Combine sugar and pectin in a saucepan or a microwaveable bowl. Stir in water and bring to a boil.

Combine herb(s), oil and ascorbic acid in a food processor and pulse a few times. With the motor running, slowly pour the hot syrup over the herb mixture so that it emulsifies. Continue mixing for at least 1 minute, or until all chlorophyll has been released (the mixture should be deep green).

Strain the emulsion through cheesecloth, squeezing hard to remove all liquid. Refrigerate in a small airtight container or, better yet, covered with plastic wrap pressed tightly against the emulsion. The emulsion will keep for 3 to 4 days.

Yield: 125 mL (½ cup)

CITRUS EMULSION

125 mL (½ cup) citrus juice
2 large eggs
4 large egg yolks
75 g (2.7 oz) granulated sugar
2.5 g (1¼) gelatin leaves, bloomed
75 g (2.7 oz) unsalted butter

Scald juice in a heavy saucepan. Combine eggs, egg yolks and sugar in another saucepan; whisk vigorously by hand until the mixture is smooth and creamy.

Pour juice into the egg mixture a little at a time, whisking constantly. Bring the mixture to a boil, stirring constantly to prevent scorching. Remove from heat and add gelatin. Cool the mixture over an ice-water bath until it reaches body temperature.

Place butter in a food processor. With the motor running, slowly pour in egg mixture a little at a time so that it emulsifies and thickens. Refrigerate for up to 1 week. The emulsion can be frozen in a plastic container with a tight-fitting lid for up to 1 month. Thaw frozen emulsion overnight in the fridge.

Note: Serve cold as a filling or warm as a sauce. For best results, place emulsion in a microwaveable dish and warm in 15-second intervals. Stir between intervals. Repeat until the mixture is warmed.

Yield: 455 g (16.4 oz)

VARIATION:

LEMON-APPLE EMULSION
Use 50% lemon juice with 50% apple juice concentrate instead of 100% lemon juice.

Citrus dressing

75 g (2.7 oz) granulated sugar
1.25 mL (¼ tsp) powdered pectin
200 mL (¾ cup + 1 Tbsp) fruit stock, page 151
50 mL (3 Tbsp + 1 tsp) lemon juice
2 vanilla beans, split lengthwise and seeds scraped
2 g (1) gelatin leaf, bloomed

In a saucepan, mix sugar and pectin. Add stock, juice and vanilla seeds, and bring to a rolling boil, stirring quickly with a whisk to prevent clumping. Remove from heat and add gelatin. Refrigerate. The dressing will keep for 1 week in the fridge or up to 1 month in the freezer.

Note: If dressing is too set to use, heat a small portion in a microwave oven. Add hot dressing to the rest and mix to dissolve.

Yield: 330 mL (1¼ cups + 2 Tbsp)

Gelées

160 mL (⅔ cup) liquid
3 g (1½) gelatin leaves, bloomed

Line a shallow 12.5 × 22.5 cm (5 × 9″) loaf pan or container with plastic wrap.

Heat ⅓ liquid in a microwave oven. Add gelatin and stir until dissolved. Add remaining ⅔ liquid and combine. Pour the mixture into the pan, and refrigerate or freeze according to the individual recipe until set. Cut into shapes.

Yield: 160 mL (⅔ cup)

VARIATIONS:

CABERNET FRANC ICEWINE GELÉE
Substitute ruby port if Cabernet Franc icewine is not available.

ROSEHIP GELÉE
Steep 1 bag rosehip tea in 175 mL (⅔ cup + 1 Tbsp) water.

SALMONBERRY GELÉE
Use 160 mL (⅔ cup) salmonberry purée, or substitute golden or red raspberries.

CHOCOLATE GELÉE
50 mL (3 Tbsp + 1 tsp) water
25 g (0.9 oz) unsweetened cocoa powder, sifted
70 g (2.5 oz) granulated sugar
4 g (2) gelatin leaves, bloomed

Bring water to a boil in a small pot. In a bowl, thoroughly mix cocoa with sugar; pour it over water. Bring the mixture back to a boil. Remove from heat, strain and add gelatin.

Pour the mixture into a container with a tight-fitting lid, and refrigerate.

Reductions and compotes

FRUIT REDUCTION

15 mL (1 Tbsp) granulated sugar
1.25 mL (¼ tsp) powdered pectin
10 mL (2 tsp) honey
200 mL (¾ cup + 1 Tbsp) fruit juice (or purée), page 151

In a small bowl, mix sugar and pectin. In a small saucepan, dissolve honey in juice. Pour sugar mixture into honey mixture, stirring quickly with a whisk to prevent clumping. Cook until the mixture is thick and syrupy. Strain, if necessary. Keep warm until serving time, or refrigerate for up to 1 week.

Yield: 125 mL (½ cup)

VARIATIONS:

CITRUS REDUCTION
170 mL (⅔ cup + 2 tsp) orange juice
30 mL (2 Tbsp) lemon juice

PORT REDUCTION
Use port in place of fruit juice.

RASPBERRY–RED PEPPER REDUCTION

100 mL (⅓ cup + 1 Tbsp) raspberry
    purée, page 151

100 mL (⅓ cup + 1 Tbsp) red pepper
    purée

To make the red pepper purée,
roast 1 medium red pepper in a
180°C (350°F) oven until skin is
wrinkled all over and flesh is soft.
Remove from the oven and place in
a heavy-duty sealable plastic bag.
Seal the top so that no steam can
escape. Cool, remove from bag, and
peel pepper with the back of a paring knife. Discard skin, membranes
and seeds. Purée roasted pepper
in a food processor.

WINE REDUCTION

Use the same recipe and procedure
as for fruit reduction but omit pectin. Without pectin, wine reductions
typically need to be cooked for
longer.

Sorbets

BASIC METHOD

In a saucepan, combine sugar and
powdered pectin (and unsweetened
cocoa powder for chocolate sorbet).
Add water and bring the mixture to
a boil, either on the stovetop or in a
microwave oven. Make sure the mixture is transparent; if it is milky, the
pectin is not completely "cooked."
Stir in fruit juice(s) and/or wine (and
chopped chocolate, if indicated, for

chocolate sorbets). Mix thoroughly.
If necessary, strain and discard
solids. Refrigerate the mixture overnight. Churn using a regular ice
cream machine and keep frozen.
Sorbet will keep up to 1 week.

VARIATIONS:

APRICOT SORBET

140 g (5 oz) granulated sugar

2 mL (⅓ tsp) powdered pectin

110 mL (⅓ cup + 1 Tbsp + 2 tsp)
    water

250 mL (1 cup) apricot purée,
    page 151
    Yield: 500 mL (2 cups)

CACTUS PEAR SORBET

75 g (2.7 oz) granulated sugar

3.75 mL (¾ tsp) powdered pectin

145 mL (½ cup + 1 Tbsp + 2 tsp)
    water

290 mL (1 cup + 2 Tbsp + 2 tsp)
    cactus pear purée, page 151
    Yield: 500 mL (2 cups)

CARROT SORBET

80 g (2.9 oz) granulated sugar

2 mL (⅓ tsp) powdered pectin

125 mL (½ cup) water

300 mL (1 cup + 3 Tbsp + 2 tsp)
    carrot purée
    Yield: 500 mL (2 cups)

CHOCOLATE SORBET

70 g (2.5 oz) granulated sugar

14 g (0.5 oz) unsweetened cocoa
    powder

5 mL (1 tsp) powdered pectin

315 mL (1¼ cups + 1 tsp) water

40 g (1.4 oz) corn syrup

75 g (2.7 oz) 70% cocoa dark choco-
    late, finely chopped
    Yield: 500 mL (2 cups)

GREEN APPLE–SKIN SORBET

50 g (1.9 oz) granulated sugar

1.25 mL (¼ tsp) powdered pectin

105 mL (⅓ cup + 1 Tbsp + 1 tsp)
    water

zest and juice of ½ lime

5 large organic Granny Smith apples,
    skin only, leaving 0.5 cm (3/16")
    flesh on the skin

Mix sugar and pectin, add
water and zest and bring to a boil.
Remove from heat, strain, and add
juice. Place apple skin in a high-
speed blender and pour syrup on
top. Blend until the mixture reaches
a uniform purée.

Yield: 500 mL (2 cups)

GUAVA SORBET

85 g (3.1 oz) granulated sugar

2 mL (⅓ tsp) powdered pectin

125 mL (½ cup) water

300 mL (1 cup + 3 Tbsp + 1 tsp)
    guava purée, page 151
    Yield: 500 mL (2 cups)

LEMON SORBET

110 g (4 oz) granulated sugar

2.5 mL (½ tsp) powdered pectin

190 mL (¾ cup + 2 tsp) water

200 mL (¾ cup + 1 Tbsp) lemon juice
    Yield: 500 mL (2 cups)

MANGO SORBET

125 g (4.5 oz) granulated sugar

2.5 mL (½ tsp) powdered pectin

125 mL (½ cup) water

250 mL (1 cup) mango purée,
    page 151

ORANGE SORBET

85 g (3.1 oz) granulated sugar

2 mL (⅓ tsp) powdered pectin

85 mL (⅓ cup + 1 tsp) water

350 mL (1¼ cups + 3 Tbsp + 1 tsp)
  orange juice (navel or mandarin),
  page 151

Yield: 500 mL (2 cups)

PEACH SORBET

85 g (3.1 oz) granulated sugar

2 mL (⅓ tsp) powdered pectin

85 mL (⅓ cup + 1 tsp) water

330 mL (1¼ cups + 2 Tbsp) peach
  purée, page 151

Yield: 500 mL (2 cups)

PINK GRAPEFRUIT SORBET

85 g (3.1 oz) granulated sugar

2 mL (⅓ tsp) powdered pectin

85 mL (⅓ cup + 1 tsp) water

350 mL (1¼ cups + 3 Tbsp + 1 tsp)
  pink grapefruit juice, page 151

Yield: 500 mL (2 cups)

YAM SORBET

250 g (9.1 oz) roasted yam purée

120 g (4.3 oz) granulated sugar

3.75 mL (¾ tsp) powdered pectin

150 mL (½ cup + 2 Tbsp) water

To make roasted yam purée, prick a yam all over with a fork and wrap in aluminum foil. Bake in a 180°C (350°F) oven until a knife inserted in the flesh comes out easily. Cut yam in half and scrape flesh from skin. Discard skin. Push flesh through a fine-mesh strainer or tamis, or mash finely.

Yield: 500 mL (2 cups)

Cream fillings

PASTRY CREAM

250 mL (1 cup) whole milk

60 g (2.1 oz) granulated sugar

25 g (0.9 oz) custard powder or
  cornstarch

1 large egg

Scald milk with ½ the sugar in a heavy saucepan.

In a bowl, vigorously mix the other ½ of the sugar with custard powder and egg, by hand with a whisk, until the mixture is smooth and creamy.

Pour hot milk into the egg mixture a little at a time, whisking constantly. Strain this combined mixture back into the saucepan.

Cook the mixture over high heat until it forms bubbles and thickens, stirring constantly with a wire whisk to prevent scorching. Remove from heat, transfer to a clean container, and cover immediately with plastic wrap pressed right against the cream. Using the sharp point of a knife, puncture about 6 holes to allow steam to escape. Cool and refrigerate. The cream will keep refrigerated for 3 to 4 days. (It does not freeze very successfully; for more information, read about gelatinization on page 87.)

Yield: 375 g (13.6 oz)

ALMOND CREAM

120 g (4.3 oz) almonds, blanched

15 g (0.6 oz) custard powder or
  cornstarch

180 g (6.4 oz) icing sugar

150 g (5.3 oz) unsalted butter,
  softened

2 large eggs

Using a food processor, grind almonds, custard powder and sugar to a fine powder. Add butter and process until the mixture is creamy and well combined. Add eggs and mix just long enough to incorporate them; be very careful not to overmix or you will not achieve the desired texture once baked. Pour into a clean container with a tight-fitting lid and refrigerate. Almond cream can also be successfully frozen.

Use almond cream as is or make a mix of 100% almond cream with 50% pastry cream. The cream will keep refrigerated for up to 1 week. Frozen almond-pastry cream can be stored for up to 3 months.

Yield: 454 g (1 lb)

Décors

CARAMEL

90 g (3.2 oz) granulated sugar
20 g (0.7 oz) corn syrup
30 mL (2 Tbsp) water

Combine sugar, syrup and water in a saucepan; cook over high heat until the mixture is caramel in colour. Remove from heat. See individual recipes for instructions on processing caramel into specific décors. For more information, read about caramelization on page 123.

Yield: 100 g (3.6 oz)

NUT PRALINE

75 g (2.7 oz) granulated sugar
30 mL (2 Tbsp) water
75 g (2.7 oz) nuts, chopped

Combine sugar and water; bring to a boil. Cook over high heat until syrup is thick, or reaches 121°C (250°F). Add nuts and continue cooking, stirring constantly, until the mixture is light caramel in colour. Pour onto a silicone mat or silicone paper and allow to cool.

Break praline into small pieces. Grind in a food processor until the paste is homogenized and the consistency of chunky peanut butter. Transfer to a plastic container with a tight-fitting lid and refrigerate for up to several months.

Yield: 150 g (5.3 oz)

CARAMELIZED NUTS

100 g (3.6 oz) nuts
125 mL (½ cup) simple syrup, page 152

Preheat the oven to 180°C (350°F). Combine nuts and syrup and bring to a boil (using a stove or a microwave oven). Boil for 1 to 2 minutes and strain. Discard syrup.

Spread nuts on a silicone mat or silicone paper and bake for 10 to 15 minutes, or until golden brown. Cool and store in an airtight container.

Yield: 100 g (3.6 oz)

CROUSTILLANT

10 g (0.4 oz) seeds
10 g (0.4 oz) all-purpose flour
50 g (1.9 oz) nuts, finely chopped
60 g (2.1 oz) granulated sugar
1.25 mL (¼ tsp) powdered pectin
30 mL (2 Tbsp) milk
25 g (0.9 oz) corn syrup
50 g (1.9 oz) salted butter

In a bowl, mix seeds, flour and nuts. Set aside.

Mix sugar and pectin in a saucepan. Add milk, syrup and butter and cook until the mixture reaches 112°C (230°F). Stir in the dry ingredients and mix well. Pour the batter onto a silicone mat. Cover with another silicone mat. Roll the batter to a thickness of about 2 mm (⅛″). Freeze.

To bake, preheat the oven to 180°C (350°F). Cut the frozen batter into shapes (refer to individual recipe for specific directions). Bake for 5 to 10 minutes (depending on size of shapes), or until golden.

Yield: 235 g (8.5 oz)

CARROT CHIPS

1 carrot, peeled
150 mL (½ cup + 2 Tbsp) simple syrup, page 152

Preheat the oven to 100°C (200°F).

Using a peeler, slice carrot into long, unbroken strands. (It is easy to shorten them later, if needed.) Cut slices into thin strips.

Bring syrup to a boil. Remove from heat and drop in carrot strands. Soak for just a few minutes. When carrots start to become translucent, drain syrup. Place carrots on a silicone mat and bake for 30 to 60 minutes. Check carrots halfway through cooking time; when carrots are dry on one side, turn them and dry the other side. Cool dried carrots and store in an airtight container.

Yield: about 24 chips

CRYSTALLIZED LEAVES

150 g (5.3 oz) granulated sugar
48 leaves
2 large egg whites

Pour sugar into a shallow bowl. Lightly brush leaves with egg whites on both sides then press into sugar. Place them on a microwaveable dish and cook on high in 15-second intervals. Turn leaves between intervals to dry both sides. As leaves begin to dry, cook for shorter and shorter intervals. Store in an airtight container until needed.

Yield: 48 leaves

Resource List

EQUIPMENT

The stores listed below provide and/or carry most of the special tools and equipment listed in this book, including silicone mats, pastry combs, Japanese mandoline/slicers, ice cream scoops, ring moulds, thermometers, digital scales, etc.

A Cook's Wares
1-800-915-9788
www.cookswares.com

Crate & Barrel
1-800-967-6696
www.crateandbarrel.com

Dean & Deluca
1-877-826-9246
www.deandeluca.com

Dudson Fine China
www.Dudson.com

Home Outfitters
www.hbc.com

JB Prince
1-800-473-0577
www.jbprince.com

Macy's
1-800-289-6229
www.macys.com

Sur La Table
1-800-243-0852
www.surlatable.com

Williams-Sonoma
1-877-812-6235
www.williams-sonoma.com

INGREDIENTS

Chocolate and specialty ingredients such as gelatin leaves, pectin, caramel powder, infused oils, fleur de sel and other CuliScience ingredients.

DC Duby Wild Sweets
604-277-6102
www.dcduby.com

D·C·D·U·B·Y
Wild sweets

The Virtual Boutique | The Chefs | The Story

Dominique and Cindy Duby are the chefs / owners of critically acclaimed DC DUBY Wild Sweets, an exotic chocolates atelier and virtual boutique located at www.dcduby.com. The Dubys combine artistry and science, and their true passion lies in scientific research aimed at expanding the palette of flavours and ingredients available to patissiers and chocolatiers. They are part of a growing group of chefs who see science and psychology as integral to the modern food experience. Their methodology is based on "molecular gastronomy" or the application of scientific techniques to the understanding and improvement of small-scale artisan food production. Dominique and Cindy take their chocolate seriously and spend considerable time researching new ways to provide their customers with superlative taste experiences. They work with food scientists to research, develop and implement techniques to create new tastes and textures. The results of their work include such novel concepts as "tasting" science kits and an annual limited-release chocolates collection—part of their commitment to developing complex, multi-sensory approaches to experiencing food. While there's a strong scientific foundation to their work, the Dubys—who call their science-based approach culinary constructivism—don't believe in putting science above art. Their unique approach is showcased in their Wild Sweets Theatre—a multi-sensory, laboratory-like Chocolate Education Centre with a state-of-the-art teaching kitchen that offers "edutaining" and interactive sweet, savoury and pairing sessions. For more information on the creativity of Wild Sweets, please visit www.dcduby.com.

"Beautiful . . . gorgeous and delicious" | **CNN American Morning**
"Atomic chefs . . . a testament to relentless creativity" | **McLeans' Magazine**
"Really cool . . . unique . . . chocolates you will never forget" | **NBC Today Weekend**
"A multisensory chocolate experience in a more-sophisticated-way than 9½ Weeks" | **Daily Candy**
"Out-of-this-world chocolates" | **Globe & Mail**

Index

Almond and cherry frangipane, 32
almond cream, 155
almond-cherry blancmanges, 32
alpine strawberry and basil-infused
    pavés, 149
alpine strawberry compote, 28
anise and chickpea biscotti, 138
anise French toast, maple and, 14
apple, apricot and pine nut topping, 23
apple and eggplant croûte with apple
    butter, cranberry compote and
    lemon-poached apples, 78
apple butter, 78
apple chips, 36
apple pasta, crispy, 124
apple salad, 103
apple softcake with dark chocolate and
    cinnamon soup, 103
apple–lemon thyme reduction, 78
apples, lemon-poached, 78
apples, slow-roasted Fuji, 56
apricot, cherry and pistachio topping, 23
apricot soup, 49
apricot-and-chanterelle wonton with
    tamago roll and plum sauce, 44
apricots, caramelized, 48
apricots, roasted, 100
avocado pudding, 39

Baked blue cheesecake mousse with
    rhubarb compote and celery confit, 66
baked chocolate mousse with mandarin
    oranges and anise seed croustillant, 94
bananas, caramelized, 99
bark, zesty chocolate, 103
basic canapé dough, 21
basic tuiles, 31
basil-infused pavés, alpine strawberry
    and, 149
basil soup, orange and, 28
beet brunoise, roasted, 15
beignets, crabapple, 36
biscotti. See cookies
black pepper softcake with lemon
    verbena–pistachio ravioli and
    cherry reduction, 62
black truffle brown butter, orange and, 108
blancmanges, cherry-almond, 32
blinis, warm chocolate, 112
blood orange and fleur de sel pavés, 145
blueberry pavés, lavender-infused and, 144

blueberry thins, 14
borage honey dentelles, grapefruit and, 134
Brazil nut harlequins, cashew and, 148
bread pudding, pan-fried, 88
brunoise, roasted beet, 15
buckwheat honey gingersnaps, 134

Cabbage, sweet Savoy, 31
CAKES:
    carrot, 84
    chocolate custard, 99
    maple whisky, 52
    pound, 48
Cambozola fondant, 128
Canadian maple whisky truffles, 143
canapé dough, basic, 21
CANAPE TOPPINGS:
    apple, apricot and pine nut, 23
    apricot, cherry and pistachio, 23
    fennel confit, lemon and almond, 23
    fig, orange and walnut, 23
candied black olives, 131
candied dates, 48
candied grapefruit zest, 39
candied squash, 76
candied tapioca pearls, 120
caramel, 156
caramel powder, 72
caramel sauce, 88
caramel-cassis sauce, 36
caramel-poblano parfait, 81
caramelization, 123
caramelized apricots, 48
caramelized bananas, 99
caramelized nuts, 156
cardamom truffles, carrot and, 143
carpaccio, nectarine, 71
carpaccio, strawberry, 131
carrot and cardamom truffles, 143
carrot and plum sauce, 56
carrot cake with peach-ginger cream and
    Saskatoon berry compote, 84
carrot chips, 156
carrot pudding with roasted beet brunoise
    and sauce, 15
cashew and Brazil nut harlequins, 148
cassis-caramel sauce, 36
celery and walnut croustillant
    chocolates, 148

celery confit and celery chips, 69
chanterelle-and-apricot wonton, 44
cherimoya frappé, maple wine and, 120
cherry frangipane, almond and, 32
cherry-almond blancmange over
    frangipane and crème fraîche soup, 32
chestnut moelleux with slow-roasted Fuji
    apples and pear tempura, 56
chiboust, orange, 71
chickpea biscotti, anise and, 138
chicon, orange-braised, 88
chicory ice cream, 88
chili matches, crispy, 81
CHIPS:
    apple, 36
    carrot, 156
    celery, 69
    peach, 84
chocolate, dark, and cinnamon soup, 103
chocolate, dark, "six façons", 115
chocolate, milk, and orange parfait, 108
chocolate, white, and cranberry
    risotto, 100
chocolate, white, and rice milk flan, 96
chocolate, white, and yogurt mousse
    mille-feuille, 111
chocolate croquette, 116
chocolate custard cake and exotic fruit
    gelée and caramelized bananas, 99
chocolate décor, 63, 111, 113
chocolate foam, 115
chocolate softcake, 108, 116
chocolate sorbet with meringue, 116
chocolate spaghetti, 120
chocolate spring roll, 104
chocolate sticks, 99
CHOCOLATES:
    alpine strawberry and basil-infused
        pavés, 149
    blood orange and fleur de sel
        pavés, 145
    Canadian maple whisky truffles, 143
    carrot and cardamom truffles, 143
    cashew and Brazil nut harlequins, 148
    celery and walnut croustillant, 148
    chokecherry and kriek pavés, 144
    corn, walnut and malt croquants, 149
    fruit and crystallized herb
        mendiants, 144
    wild blueberry and lavender-infused
        pavés, 144

chocoufflé, 115
chokecherry and kriek pavés, 144
churning/overrun, 35
cinnamon soup, dark chocolate and, 103
citrus crackers, 71
citrus dressing, 153
citrus emulsion, 152
citrus oil, 151
clafoutis, Concord grape, 31
coagulation, 24
cocoa sticks, 108
coconut curry foam, 76
coconut leaves, crispy, 20
coconut milk sabayon, 47
coconut salad and honey dressing, 47
COMPOTES, 153
    alpine strawberry, 28
    cranberry, 78
    fireweed honey–roasted tomato, 81
    pear and icewine, 61
    physalis, 16
    quince, 52
    rhubarb, 66
    Saskatoon berry, 84
    yellow pepper and mango, 112
Concord grape clafoutis with sweet Savoy
    cabbage and warm grapes, 31
CONFITS:
    celery, 69
    fennel, 23
    red lentil, 124
COOKIES:
    anise and chickpea biscotti, 138
    basic tuiles, 31
    blueberry thins, 14
    buckwheat honey gingersnaps, 134
    chocolate sticks, 99
    cocoa sticks, 108
    coriander and orange oil
        gaufrettes, 138
    grapefruit and borage honey
        dentelles, 134
    lemon and mint oil sucrées, 137
    orange blossom and fennel
        financiers, 138
    orange blossom fingers, 120
    rhubarb tuiles, 66
    rose water tuiles, 32
    sunflower and ginseng macaroons, 139
    Szechwan pepper cocoa barks, 134
    tamarind and pumpkin seed sablés, 137

    vanilla cookies, 100
    wattle seed and walnut wedges, 137
    wild rice flour thins, 16
coriander and orange oil gaufrettes, 138
corn, walnut and malt croquants, 149
crabapple beignets, 36
crackers, citrus, 71
cranberry compote, 78
cranberry risotto, creamy white
    chocolate and, 100
CREAM FILLINGS, 155
    almond, 155
    peach-ginger, 84
    pastry, 155
creaming, 140
creamy avocado pudding with pink grape-
    fruit reduction and candied zest, 39
creamy white chocolate and cranberry
    risotto with roasted apricots, 100
crème fraîche soup, 32
crèmes renversées with crabapple beignets
    and cassis-caramel sauce, 36
crépaze, lemon, 124
crispy apple pasta, 124
crispy chili matches, 81
crispy coconut leaves, 20
crispy rice croquant, 16
CROQUANTS:
    corn, walnut and malt, 149
    crispy rice, 16
    pumpkin seed, 47
    strawberry, 51
croquette, chocolate, 116
croustillant, 156
croûte, apple and eggplant, 78
crunchy chocolate spring roll with mint
    and mango salad, 104
crystallized herb mendiants, fruit and, 144
crystallized leaves, 156
custard, lavender, 14

Dark chocolate "six façons," 115
dark chocolate and cinnamon soup, 103
dates, candied, 48
date mousse pound cake with caramelized
    apricots and icewine foam, 48
DECORS, 155
    chocolate, 63
    white chocolate, 111, 113

deep-fried ravioli and pasta strands, 62
dentelles. See cookies
dressing, citrus, 153
dressing, honey, 47

Eggplant croûte, apple and, 78
emulsification, 65
EMULSIONS, 152
    citrus, 152
    herb, 152
    lemon balm, 112
    lemon verbena–pistachio, 62
    pistachio, 96
exotic fruit foam, 99
exotic fruit salad with guava sauce and
    phyllo galettes, 51

Fennel confit, lemon and almond
    topping, 23
fennel financiers, orange blossom and, 138
fermentation, 19
feuille de brick mille-feuilles, 111
fig, orange and walnut topping, 23
financiers. See cookies
fireweed honey–roasted tomatoes and
    compote, 81
flan, red curry squash, 76
flan, white chocolate and rice milk, 96
fleur de sel pavés, blood orange and, 145
foaming, 107
FOAMS AND SABAYONS:
    chocolate, 115
    coconut curry, 76
    coconut milk, 47
    exotic fruit, 99
    icewine, 48
    rhubarb, 66
fondant, Cambozola, 128
frangipane, almond and cherry, 32
frappé, maple wine and cherimoya, 120
French toast, 14
frites, polenta, 128
fruit and crystallized herb mendiants, 144
fruit juice and fruit purée, 151
fruit reduction, 153
fruit salad, 51
fruit stock, 151

Galette, phyllo, 51
galette, riso, 127
gaufrettes. See cookies

gelatinization, 87
GELEES, 153
    icewine, 47
ginger-braised Hon pears and
    reduction, 127
ginger-peach cream, 84
gingersnaps. *See* cookies
ginseng macaroons, sunflower and, 139
gnocchi, spiced squash, 76
goat cheese ice cream, 52
grapes, warm, 31
grape clafoutis, Concord, 31
grapefruit and borage honey dentelles, 134
grapefruit reduction, pink, 39
grapefruit zest, candied, 39
grilled pear steak with polenta frites and
    orange-tarragon sauce, 128
guava sauce, 51

Harlequins. *See* chocolates
herb emulsion, 152
herb oil, 151

Ice cream and sorbets, 154–156
    chicory ice cream, 88
    chocolate sorbet, 116
    goat cheese ice cream, 52
    rice pudding ice cream, 16
    vanilla ice cream, 20
icewine compote, pear and, 61
icewine foam, 48
icewine gelée with coconut milk sabayon
    and pumpkin seed croquant, 47
infused oils, 151

Juice, fruit, 151
juice, pineapple, 20

Kriek pavés, chokecherry and, 144

Lavender custard, 14
lavender-infused pavés, wild
    blueberry and, 144
lemon and mint oil sucrées, 137
lemon balm emulsion, 112
lemon crépaze with red lentil confit and
    crispy apple pasta, 124
lemon thyme–apple reduction, 78
lemon verbena–pistachio emulsion, 62
lemon-poached apples, 78
lentil confit, red, 124

Macaroons. *See* cookies
malt croquants, corn and walnut and, 149
malt drink, 117
mango compote, yellow pepper and, 112
mango fillet, smoked, 61
mango gratin, 61
mango salad, mint and, 104
maple and anise French toast with
    lavender custard, 14
maple whisky cake, 52
maple whisky sauce, 52
maple wine and cherimoya frappé with
    orange blossom fingers, 120
mascarpone mousse, 28
meringue, 116
meringues, steamed, 108
milk chocolate and orange parfait with
    steamed meringues and orange and
    black truffle brown butter, 108
mille-feuilles, feuille de brick, 111
mint and mango salad, 104
mint oil sucrées, lemon and, 137
moelleux, chestnut, 56
MOUSSES:
    blue cheesecake, 66
    chocolate, 94
    date, 48
    mascarpone, 28
    white chocolate and yogurt, 111

Nectarine carpaccio, 71
nuts, caramelized, 156
nut praline, 156

Oils:
    citrus, 151
    herb, 151
    infused, 151
olives, candied black, 131
orange, blood, and fleur de sel pavés, 145
orange and basil soup, alpine strawberry
    compote and mascarpone mousse, 28
orange and black truffle brown butter, 108
orange blossom and fennel financiers, 138
orange blossom fingers, 120
orange chiboust with nectarine carpaccio
    and citrus crackers, 71
orange oil gaufrettes, coriander and, 138

orange parfait, milk chocolate and, 108
orange-braised chicon, 88
orange-tarragon sauce, 128
overrun/churning, 35

Pan-fried bread pudding with
    orange-braised chicon and chicory
    ice cream, 88
parfait, milk chocolate and orange, 108
parfait, poblano-caramel, 81
pastry cream, 155
pavés. *See* chocolates
pea shoot salad, 61
peach chips, 84
peach-ginger cream, 84
pears, ginger-braised Hon, 127
pear and icewine compote with smoked
    mango fillet and sweet pea shoot
    salad, 61
pear lace, 127
pear salad, 59
pear steak, grilled, 128
pear tempura, 56
phyllo galette, 51
physalis compote, 16
pineapple juice, 20
pineapple roast, spiced, 20
pistachio emulsion, 96
pistachio–lemon verbena emulsion, 62
plating, 10
plum sauce, 44
plum sauce, carrot and, 56
plum wine–poached raisins, 59
plums, poached, 44
poblano-caramel parfait with fireweed
    honey–roasted tomatoes and chili
    matches, 81
polenta frites, 128
pound cake, 48
praline, nut, 156
PROCESSES:
    caramelization, 123
    churning/overrun, 35
    coagulation, 24
    creaming, 140
    emulsification, 65
    fermentation, 19
    foaming, 107
    gelatinization, 87
    plating, 10
    tempering, 147

PUDDINGS:
avocado, 39
carrot, 15
pan-fried bread, 88
rice, 16
wheat berry, 131
pumpkin seed croquant, 47
pumpkin seed sablés, tamarind and, 137
purée, fruit, 151

Quince compote, 52
quince-filled maple whisky cake with goat
cheese ice cream, 52

Raisins, plum wine–poached 59
ravioli, lemon verbena–pistachio, 62
red curry squash flan with gnocchi and
coconut curry foam, 76
red lentil confit, 124
REDUCTIONS, 153
cherry, 62
fruit, 153
ginger-braised Hon pear, 127
lemon thyme–apple, 78
white balsamic vinegar, 72
rhubarb compote, 66
rhubarb foam, 66
rhubarb tuiles, 66
rice, crispy croquant, 16
rice milk flan, white chocolate and, 96
rice paper salad, 96
rice pudding ice cream, 16
rice pudding with physalis compote, 16
riso galette with ginger-braised Hon
pears, 127
risotto, creamy white chocolate and
cranberry, 100
roasted apricots, 100
roasted beet brunoise and sauce, 15
rose water tuiles, 32

Sabayon. See foams and sabayons
sablés. See cookies
Saskatoon berry compote, 84
SALADS:
apple, 103
coconut, 47
exotic fruit, 51
mint and mango, 104

pea shoot, 61
pear, 59
rice paper, 96
SAUCES:
caramel, 88
carrot and plum, 56
cassis-caramel, 36
guava, 51
maple whisky, 52
orange-tarragon, 128
plum, 44
roasted beet, 15
sweet and sour, 104
sesame glass, 53
simple syrup, 152
slow-roasted Fuji apples, 56
SOFTCAKES:
apple, 103
black pepper, 62
chocolate, 108, 116
sorbets. See ice cream and sorbets
SOUPS:
apricot, 49
crème fraîche, 32
dark chocolate and cinnamon, 103
orange and basil, 28
spaghetti, chocolate, 120
spiced pineapple roast and juice, 20
spiced pineapple roast with chocolate
softies, 20
spiced smoked mango fillets, 61
spiced squash gnocchi, 76
spring roll, crunchy chocolate, 104
spring roll wrapper garnish, 78
squash, candied, 76
squash flan, red curry, 76
squash gnocchi, spiced, 76
steamed meringues, 108
stock, fruit, 151
strawberry, alpine, and basil-infused
pavés, 149
strawberry, alpine, compote, 28
strawberry carpaccio, 131
strawberry croquant, 51
sucrées. See cookies
sunflower and ginseng macaroons, 139

sweet and sour sauce, 104
Szechwan pepper cocoa barks, 134
syrup, simple, 152

Tamago roll, 44
tamarind and pumpkin seed sablés, 137
tapioca pearls, candied, 120
tarragon-orange sauce, 128
tempering, 147
tempura, pear, 56
tomatoes, fireweed honey–roasted, 81
truffles. See chocolates
TUILES:
basic, 31
rhubarb, 66
rose water, 32

Vanilla cookies, 100
vanilla ice cream, 20

Walnut croquants, corn and malt and, 149
walnut croustillant chocolates, celery
and, 148
walnut wedges, wattle seed and, 137
warm chocolate blinis with yellow pepper
and mango compote, 112
warm Concord grapes, 31
wattle seed and walnut wedges, 137
wheat berry pudding with candied black
olives, 131
white balsamic vinegar reduction, 72
white chocolate and cranberry risotto, 100
white chocolate and rice milk flan with
pistachio emulsion, 96
white chocolate and yogurt mousse
mille-feuille, 111
white chocolate décor, 111, 113
wild blueberry and lavender-infused
pavés, 144
wild rice flour thins, 16
wine pairing, 55
wonton, apricot-and-chanterelle, 44

Yellow pepper and mango compote, 112
yogurt mousse mille-feuille, white
chocolate and, 111

Zest, candied, 39
zesty chocolate bark, 103